PROGRESSIVE REVELATION: God's disclosure of truth about His coming kingdom

Bill F. Korver

www.metakoi.com

Copyright 2021 Bill F. Korver. 3rd Edition. All rights reserved. No portion of this book may be reproduced, stored in a retrieval system, or transmitted in any form or by any other means – electronic, mechanical, photocopy, recording or other – except for brief quotations in printed reviews, without the written consent of the publisher.

Published by Metakoi Publishing and Lightning Source (a subsidiary of Ingram Content Group), 1246 Heil Quaker Boulevard, La Verrgne, TN USA 37086

All scripture quotations, unless otherwise indicated, are taken from the Holy Bible, New American Standard (NAS) version, copyright by the Lockman Foundation.

Korver, Bill F.

Progressive Revelation: God's disclosure of truth about His coming kingdom

ISBN: 978-0-9905783-2-1

1. Bible Study 2. Theology 3. Korver, Bill

Printed in the United States of America

Contents

INTRODUCTION 5
Chapter 1: AN INTRODUCTION TO PROGRESSIVE REVELATION 7
Chapter 2: THE THEME OF THE BIBLE..19
Chapter 3: DIFFERENT ASPECTS OF GOD'S KINGDOM 31
Chapter 4: PEOPLE, PROMISES and PERIODS 39
Chapter 5: FROM EDEN TO UR 55
Chapter 6: FROM UR TO SINAI 63
Chapter 7: A KINGDOM OF PRIESTS..75
Chapter 8: FROM JERUSALEM TO BABYLON AND BACK......................89
Chapter 9: THE GOSPELS 103
Chapter 10: ACTS AND THE EPISTLES 119
Chapter 11: THE REVELATION 135
BIBLIOGRAPHY 148

INTRODUCTION

I grew up in a Christ-centered home, for which I am eternally grateful. My earliest memories include a nightly meal at the dinner table as a family. When the meal was over, we always concluded with reading a portion of scripture and prayer. As children my siblings and I participated in a Bible memorization program. By the time we were twelve years old, we had each committed hundreds of verses of Scripture to memory. We also went to church at least three times per week (Sunday morning and night and Wednesday night).

Despite those realities, the Bible seemed to me to be a loose collection of stories that in some way centered around the God who created all things. If you had asked me in those days, and for many years into my adult life, to state what was the unifying truth, the theme, of the Bible, I know for a fact I would have been at a loss to tell you.

It seemed to me that there were stories of some ancient people (e.g., Abraham, Isaac, Moses, and Daniel) found in the Old Testament. There were also stories of less ancient people (e.g., Jesus, Peter, and Paul) in the New Testament. Somehow, though foreign to me, those two sets of stories got welded together. I knew Jesus was central to the narrative because of who He is and what He did, but why all those other people and stories?

Is there a story line to the Bible? If not, why read it? If yes, what is it? This work attempts to answer those questions at a basic level. It is my hope it will piece some missing puzzle pieces together and assist the reader in seeing the of the Bible clearly and confidently.

Bill F. Korver

Chapter 1: AN INTRODUCTION TO PROGRESSIVE REVELATION

What in the world is progressive revelation and why study it? Great questions! Let's answer the "what" question first.

1A. A DEFINITION OF PROGRESSIVE REVELATION

The term "progressive revelation" comes from two ideas. "Progressive" means that something moves forward **step by step**. For example, if the entire Bible was Genesis 1:1, "In the beginning God created the heavens and the earth." We would only know a few things about God, namely that He is eternal (He was already present when time began); that He is powerful (He created things from nothing – ex nihilo) and perhaps a few more truths than those. Do you know more about God than those things? If the answer is "yes," it is because God continued to give revelation after Genesis 1:1.

The term "revelation", as used in theology and here in this chapter, refers to God disclosing to people, through the Scriptures, what they could **not otherwise know** about Him, themselves and His will. There are many things we can learn from general revelation (e.g., nature), but important concepts like sin, salvation and the possibility of and process of reconciliation would be mysteries if God had kept silent. Put together, "progressive" and "revelation" means that God revealed His Word bit by bit, over time. Instead of giving us the whole Bible at once, God revealed Himself progressively. This means that Adam knew less of God and His Word than Abraham and that Abraham had less of God's Word than you do.

2A. BIBLICAL BASIS FOR PROGRESSIVE REVELATION

Have you noticed that people can make the Bible say whatever they want it to say? Is the concept of Progressive Revelation even biblical or is just something the author invented or taken from passages of the Bible taken out of context?

I challenge you to be like the Bereans, in Acts 17:10, 11, who carefully considered what Paul taught to see if it harmonized with the rest of Scripture before accepting it as true. By the way, that approach was praised by Luke, the human writer of Acts. There is no indication that the apostle Paul took offense at the actions of those Bereans.

Progressive revelation is taught several places in the Scripture. Here are two biblical examples, each with some observations.

One is found in Hebrews 1:1-2:

(1) God, who at various times and in various ways spoke in time past to the fathers by the prophets, (2) has in these last days spoken to us by his Son...."

This text teaches us that:

- God revealed Himself in the past (1a). The King James Version of the Bible says, "...long ago" rather than "past" as does the NASB. The book of Hebrews was probably written around 68 A.D. Thus "long ago" would undoubtedly be a reference to the revelation of the Old Testament.

- God revealed Himself at different times and ways [progressively!] (1b). He did this in a variety of ways, such as dreams, visions, audible voice, angelic visitations, handwriting on a wall, and even a donkey's voice! His revelation was always clearly supernatural, not merely an impression or a "gut feeling."

- One way He spoke in the past was through the "prophets" to the "fathers" (1c). Both the terms prophets and fathers are suggestive. The term "prophets" was the normal term for individuals God spoke through in the Old Testament (though it occurs a few times in the New Testament). The term "fathers" was often used of the patriarchs – Abraham, Isaac, and Jacob. Both suggest Old Testament groups of people.

- We are in the last days (2a). The writer of Hebrews wrote those words nearly 2000 years ago, thus we must be that much closer to the end of the age now! Remember that God's timetable and timing are not the same as ours.

- God has spoken to us (2b). God did not leave us in the dark, fumbling around in spiritual darkness or ignorance. He revealed Himself. The phrases, "Thus saith the Lord", "The word of the Lord came…" and others occur thousands of times in the Bible with the majority occurring in the Old Testament.

- He has spoken to us in these last days by His Son (2b). God's final revelation was through His Son, Jesus. Consider this, the New Testament includes the four gospels, which record His birth, life, death and resurrection. Acts and the letters/epistles include the story of the birth, spread, and maturation of the church Jesus declared He would build. Finally, the Revelation is mostly a prophecy of His return to establish His kingdom on earth. Put another way, the New

Testament is God's final (special) revelation about His only (begotten) Son!

Here we observe that God used progressive revelation to give the **Old Testament** to the fathers but has concluded His revelation to us in the person of His Son, Jesus. Clearly the book of Hebrews is found in the New Testament, but it teaches that progressive revelation is an Old Testament truth (e.g., "long ago…prophets…fathers," etc.).

In Addition, we discover that progressive revelation is a New Testament reality too. We observe that Jesus employed progressive revelation when He, the Son, spoke, John 16:12-13 says:

> *(12) I still have many things to say to you, but you cannot bear them now. (13) However, when He, the Spirit of truth, has come, He will guide you into all truth; for He will not speak on His own authority, but whatever He hears He will speak; and He will tell you things to come.*

The context of John 16:12, 13 is that it occurred in the Upper Room, and most likely on Thursday night of the passion week. It was the night of Jesus' arrest and in a matter of hours He would be tried and placed on a cross. He told the eleven disciples (Judas had already left) of His impending departure. Note carefully from this passage that:

- Jesus could have told them much more than He did (12a). The implication was that the disciples, like small children, could not have "handled" all that Jesus could have revealed. Much like young children who ask a question about a very complex or delicate issue, wise is the parent who only reveals a little bit of the truth and saves the rest of the details until an appropriate time.

- The disciples could not have understood if He had given them additional revelation (12b). Even if the disciples had possessed the physical stamina to listen to all Jesus could have told them, they did not possess the mental or spiritual ability to comprehend what He could have revealed.

- The Holy Spirit **would** come to guide the disciples into all truth (13a). Notice that Jesus said that the Spirit "would" (future tense) come and guide the disciples into all truth. Jesus did not say when this would occur, but again, because of progressive revelation, we know when this prophecy was fulfilled. It occurred in Acts 2, at the birth of the church and only 53 days after than John 16. The Spirit came upon the disciples to indwell and enable them.

- The Spirit **would** hear this truth from someone else [the Father] and speak accordingly (13b). Again, the concept is future, that the Spirit "would" reveal these truths given by Someone else (the Father) and would reveal them accordingly.

- This truth included things future from that time [the New Testament] (13c). Jesus uttered these words around 30 AD. Most conservative bible scholars believe the New Testament was written between 45 and 100 AD. The writers of the New Testament did not need to have perfect memories to recall all they had seen and heard. In addition to what they had seen and heard, the Spirit of God would reveal truth to them and guide them in the inerrant recording of it.

This text teaches us that Jesus employed progressive revelation to give the **New Testament** to and through the disciples. Both Father and Son spoke progressively. So, we find that progressive revelation is certainly a Biblical doctrine.

In addition to the two foundational passages already discussed, consider the following scriptures to see if they also support the concept:

…that by revelation there was made known to me the mystery, as I wrote before in brief. <u>By referring to this, when you read you can understand my insight into the mystery of Christ, which in other generations was not made known to the sons of men, as it has now been revealed to His holy apostles</u> and prophets in the Spirit; *to be specific*, that the Gentiles are fellow heirs and fellow members of the body, and fellow partakers of the promise in Christ Jesus through the gospel, of which I was made a minister, according to the gift of God's grace which was given to me according to the working of His power. To me, the very least of all saints, this grace was given, to preach to the Gentiles the unfathomable riches of Christ, and to bring to light what is the administration of the mystery which for ages has been hidden in God who created all things. **Eph. 3:3-9** (underlining mine).

Paul states that a "mystery" is NOT what we often think. For us, a mystery is a "who done it" television show where we try to figure out who did the dastardly deed. Paul states that a mystery was something previously hidden but now revealed. That sounds exactly like progressive revelation!

Yet another passage that teaches and confirms progressive revelation is 2 Corinthians 12:1, 7:

Boasting is necessary, though it is not profitable; but I will go on to visions and revelations of the Lord. Because of the surpassing greatness of the revelations, for this reason, to keep me from exalting myself, there was given me a thorn in the flesh, a messenger of Satan to torment me—to keep me from exalting myself! **2 Cor. 12:1, 7**

And the disciples came and said to Him, "Why do You speak to them in parables?" Jesus answered them, "To you it has been granted to know the mysteries of the kingdom of heaven, but to them it has not been granted. For whoever has, to him *more* shall be given, and he will have an abundance; but whoever does not have, even what he has shall be taken away from him. **Matt. 13:10-12**

As Jesus taught in parables, a new form of teaching for Him, the disciples asked, why do you teach in this way? His response was that some rejected Him, despite clear evidence (His many miracles) yet others, such as the disciples, believed His claims. To those who believed, more revelation would be given. Again, this sounds exactly like progressive revelation.

3A. TYPES OF PROGRESSIVE REVELATION

1B. Progressive Revelation may **supplement**

Frequently later revelation **supplements** and gives a more complete understanding of the issue, person, doctrine, etc. One example is how the Bible slowly reveals more and more about who God is. In Genesis 1:1, He is God the Creator. In Genesis 2:4-25 He is the Lord God who provides for man and makes promises with him. Genesis 16:13-14 describes Him as *El Roi*, the One who sees our suffering and cares for us. On and on it goes, until finally, God comes to earth in the Person of Jesus Christ (John 1:1-14). The entire picture gives us a more complete view of God. If we only had the earlier snapshots our understanding of God would be severely limited. Thus, supplemental revelation completes earlier revelation.

Further examples of supplemental revelation would be God's revelation about angels. We learn they were present at creation (Job 38:7). We learn they guarded the entrance to the Garden of Eden after mankind was expelled. We learn that at least three of them have names (Lucifer, Michael, and Gabriel). We learn of their numbers (tens of thousands) and their activities (they are messengers of God, they minister to people, they guard the holiness of God) and much more.

Additionally, another example is God's revelation about the "seed of the woman" (Gen. 3:15) who would crush the Serpent's head. The seed was to be born in Abraham's family (Gen. 12:3); was to be born of a virgin (Isa. 7:14) and to be born in Bethlehem (Micah 5:2).

It would not be a stretch of the truth to say that every significant doctrine taught in the Bible is supplemented as one reads from beginning to end chronologically.

2B. Progressive Revelation may **Supplant**

At times, later revelation **supplants or changes** earlier revelation. One example is the Biblical teaching about food. At first, man could only eat vegetables (Gen. 1:29). Later, after the flood when God gave more revelation to man, He added meat (Gen. 9:3). Later, when God narrowed His work to one nation, Israel, He limited the meat they could eat (Lev. 11). Finally, centuries later, God revealed that we who follow Jesus may eat any food (Acts 10:14-15; 1 Tim. 4:1-5). This does not mean all foods are equally healthy or that the quantity of food consumed is not relevant.

Another example of supplanting revelation concerns the day and location of worship. In the Old Testament, God revealed to Israel that they were to corporately worship on a certain day. The Sabbath was the seventh day (technically Friday at sundown until Saturday at sundown). Further the place of worship for the great feasts was to be the temple in Jerusalem after it was built during Solomon's reign. Yet in the New Testament book of Acts the early church began to worship on Sunday, to honor the risen Savior and apparently with God's blessing. The early church soon moved from the temple to houses as the number of Gentile converts increased. In the New Testament letters, God supplanted earlier revelation by saying the day, the time and the place of corporate worship was not important, merely that it occur (see Col. 2:16-23 and Galatians 2:8-11).

Progressive revelation changed the earlier directives and clarified the later ones for us. Sometimes God introduces new things or changes things for which men are responsible.

This type of progressive revelation supplants. A note of caution regarding supplanting revelation, it is important to note that mankind is not authorized to change God's revelation, it must have clearly originated from God. He nearly always did this through prophets and apostles.

So, we have answered the question, "What is progressive revelation?" It is the step-by-step disclosure by God of what we could not otherwise know, concluded in Jesus Christ and recorded in the Bible. Progressive revelation may supplement what was written earlier and complete the teaching. Progressive revelation may also supplant earlier commands and replace them with other requirements.

Answering the "What" question also gave good answers to the "Why" question. It is clear that grasping progressive revelation will help us read the Bible more accurately and apply it more appropriately. It will also enable us to get a grip on the overall flow or theme of the Bible.

This introduction has acquainted you with progressive revelation. Reading the Bible with this realization will lead us to some accurate and marvelous conclusions.

CHAPTER 1 REVIEW/SUMMARY

1. Progressive revelation is both an Old Testament AND New Testament concept, taught in Hebrews 1:1, 2 (referring to the Old Testament) and John 16:12, 13. Additionally it is taught in Ephesians 3:3-9; 2 Corinthians 12:1, 7 and Matthew 13:10-12.

2 The definition of progressive revelation has four important parts, they are:
- God progressively, step by step, discloses truth.
- God's truth could not be known apart from His revelation of it.
- God's revelation was concluded in the person of Jesus Christ, God's final revelation.
- God's revelation was recorded in the Bible. It cannot be found in any other book (e.g., Quran, Book of Mormon, etc.).

3. There are two distinct types of progressive revelation, that which supplements (adds to earlier revelation – e.g., the character of God) and that which supplants (changes earlier revelation – e.g., dietary laws).

Chapter 2: THE THEME OF THE BIBLE

Over the years, many have attempted to summarize what ties the Bible together – its main theme or plot. This is a monumental task to say the least. The theme must be specific enough to unify the Bible yet broad enough to cover all the Bible teaches. If you were asked to state the theme of the Bible in fifteen words or less, what might be your answer?

1A. COMMONLY SUGGESTED THEMES

There are two most commonly suggested ideas for potential Bible themes. First is **salvation**; some say the Bible is all about God's work in history to bring men to heaven. This view is often referred to as "the scarlet thread of redemption" (scarlet being the color of blood – e.g., the blood of a sacrifice to redeem). The other most commonly suggested theme is **God's glory**; He works in human history to glorify Himself.

Both proposed themes can be traced throughout a great portion of the Bible, but one is too narrow while the other is too broad. It seems that the first suggestion is too narrow – the Bible is about much more than getting saved or going to heaven, or even living a sanctified life. Further, God would have had no plan in Genesis chapters 1 and 2, since people didn't need to be saved before the fall. Neither would God have a plan in Revelation 22 and eternity future when no longer will people be saved. And the latter is too general – although the goal of everything, God's glory doesn't provide a broad enough umbrella under which to place all Scripture. Is there a viable third alternative that is traceable from the earliest pages of scripture to the end? Yes. When we allow the Bible to unfold progressively, we find a clear and compelling theme. We can trace the development of this theme from Genesis through Revelation. It binds all of Scripture together.

2A. A MORE PRECISE SUGGESTED THEME

Read the following passages. and note any ideas or themes that are **repeated** or **restated**. What do you find repeated or restated?

Then God said, "Let Us make man in Our image, according to Our likeness; and let them rule over the fish of the sea and over the birds of the sky and over the cattle and over all the earth, and over every creeping thing that creeps on the earth." God created man in His own image, in the image of God He created him; male and female He created them. God blessed them; and God said to them, "Be fruitful and multiply, and fill the earth, and subdue it; and rule over the fish of the sea and over the birds of the sky and over every living thing that moves on the earth." **Gen. 1:26-28**

And God blessed Noah and his sons and said to them, "Be fruitful and multiply, and fill the earth. The fear of you and the terror of you will be on every beast of the earth and on every bird of the sky; with everything that creeps on the ground, and all the fish of the sea, into your hand they are given. Every moving thing that is alive shall be food for you; I give all to you, as *I gave* the green plant. Only you shall not eat flesh with its life, *that is*, its blood. Surely, I will require your lifeblood; from every beast I will require it. And from *every* man, from every man's brother I will require the life of man.

Whoever sheds man's blood,
By man his blood shall be
shed, For in the image of God
He made man.
"As for you, be fruitful and multiply; **Gen. 9:1-7**

When I consider Your heavens, the work of Your fingers,
The moon and the stars, which You have ordained;
What is man that You take thought of him, And
the son of man that You care for him? Yet You
have made him a little lower than God, And You
crown him with glory and majesty!
You make him to rule over the works of Your hands;
You have put all things under his feet,
All sheep and oxen,
And also the beasts of the field,

The birds of the heavens and the fish of the sea, Whatever passes through the paths of the seas.
Populate the earth abundantly and multiply in it." **Psalm 8:3-8**

There will no longer be any curse; and the throne of God and of the Lamb will be in it, and His bondservants will serve Him; they will see His face, and His name *will be* on their foreheads. And there will no longer be *any* night; and they will not have need of the light of a lamp nor the light of the sun, because the Lord God will illumine them; and they will reign forever and ever. **Rev. 22:3-5**

With just these few passages as a starting point, let me suggest the theme of the Bible. Fully stated, the Bible is about God sovereignly restoring His rule through righteous men over all the earth for His own glory. More simply, the Bible is about God's sovereign restoration of His earthly kingdom. Scripture is all about **God restoring His earthly Kingdom**. Put another way, **God acts to rule over all creation through people rightly related to Him**.

3A. THE CONCEPT OF THE KINGDOM

The Bible often uses the term "kingdom" – it is found 150 times in the New Testament alone. What is meant by "kingdom?"

A genuine kingdom must have three elements. First, someone must possess the **right** to rule. This can be seen in the following verses:

While they were listening to these things, Jesus went on to tell a parable, because He was near Jerusalem, and they supposed that the kingdom of God was going to appear immediately. So He said, "A nobleman went to a distant country to receive a kingdom for himself, and *then* return. **Luke 19:11, 12**

The ten horns which you saw are ten kings who have not yet received a kingdom, but they receive authority as kings with the beast for one hour. **Rev. 17:12**

In the Revelation passage above, it is a negative connotation to the authority, the beast (antichrist), but it does establish the truth of a right to rule. Authority, sovereignty or dominion must rest in someone's control. <u>Second</u>, a kingdom must have a **realm** over which that authority is exercised. There must be **people** (subjects) and a **place** to rule. Revelation 11:15 presents this truth:

Then the seventh angel sounded; and there were loud voices in heaven, saying, "The kingdom of the world has become *the kingdom* of our Lord and of His Christ; and He will reign forever and ever." **Rev. 11:15**

<u>Finally</u>, a kingdom requires the **exercise** of authority. The ruler's authority must be extended, or rule does not occur. Daniel 6:1-3 presents this reality:

It seemed good to Darius to appoint 120 satraps over the kingdom, that they would be in charge of the whole kingdom, and over them three commissioners (of whom Daniel was one), that these satraps might be accountable to them, and that the king might not suffer loss. Then this Daniel began distinguishing himself among the commissioners and satraps because he possessed an extraordinary spirit, and the king planned to appoint him over the entire kingdom.

Dwight Pentecost comments,

"Most significantly, in relation to Christ's earthly ministry we see that Pilate – having interrogated Christ – declared that he found no charge on which He could be condemned. Why? Though Pilate recognized that Christ claimed to be king (John 19:14-15), he declared Him without fault (vv. 4, 6) because he saw that Jesus was not actually exercising the authority He claimed for Himself."[1]

Consider the Queen of England as an example. She has a realm, the British Empire, and subjects, the people of England. However, she doesn't have the

---

1. Pentecost, J. Dwight, *Thy Kingdom Come,* (Wheaton, IL; Victor Books, 1990), 14

right to rule. That belongs to the Parliament; the Queen is a figurehead who reminds the British of their past glory. Finally, she exercises no authority because the laws made by the Parliament grant her none. She is royalty but she does not rule. This is not a genuine kingdom. On the other hand, consider King Salman (2019) of Saudi Arabia. He alone has the right to rule in his country. He makes and exercises the laws of his land. He rules over a geographic area that includes many tribal groups. This is a true kingdom. What's the difference between these two monarchs? It is the right and exercise of authority. Queen Elizabeth has none while King Salman wields both in his country. A genuine kingdom then is one in which a **ruler exercises his authority over a realm**. All three concepts, the right to rule, the realm to rule and exercise of rule are necessary for existence of a kingdom. God must have a genuine rule if the theme of the Bible revolves around His kingdom restoration. Let's review one more passage and see what we learn about God and His Kingdom. Carefully read 1 Chron. 29:11-12 below.

(11) Yours, O Lord, is the greatness, the power and glory, the victory and the majesty: For all that is in heaven and in earth is Yours; Yours is the kingdom, O Lord, and You are exalted as head over all. (12) Both riches and honor come from You, and You reign over all. In your hand is power and might; In Your hand it is to make great and to give strength to all.

Now, complete the chart below. Write in the phrases from the text above under the appropriate heading that indicates that element of God's kingdom.

Right to Rule	Realm to Rule	Exercise of Rule

Let's overview Biblical history and see if we find this kingdom theme traced throughout. Look up every reference given below to ensure they actually teach what the notes say they do. Record any questions you develop so we can discuss them.

4A. THE BIBLICAL HISTORY OF GOD'S KINGDOM[2]

Before creation, God ruled as the eternal King (1 Tim. 1:17). His Kingdom existed in the sphere of the heavenlies (Eph. 1:3; 1:20; 2:6; 3:10; 6:12). Since only God existed, He enjoyed complete exercise of His authority over His own realm. God the Father was sovereign King (Dan. 4:34-35). God the Son, although equal in person, was subordinate to the Father (1 Cor. 11:3). God the Spirit, also equal in person, was the executor of the Father's the Father's will (Gen. 1:2-3). God's eternal universal Kingdom had an

---

2. Adapted from Renald Showers, *What On Earth is God Doing?*, (Bellmawr, NJ; Friends of Israel Inc.),11-20

eternal ruler exercising sovereign authority perfectly among the Trinity.

For reasons unknown to us, God determined to localize His rule in the physical realm. God first created **angels** to serve Him and to assist His people (Job 38:4-7, Heb. 1:5-14). God then made **earth** as the place where he would exercise his localized rule (Gen. 1-2). Finally, God made **man** to reflect Him and to rule the earth for Him. God made mankind in His image and appointed them to govern earth as God's representative for God's purpose (Gen. 1:26-28; Ps. 8:3-9, Heb. 2:5-8). God's government through an appointed representative is called a **theocracy**. With God the ultimate King, man as His representative and God's Word as the law of the Kingdom, everything was very good in God's theocracy (Gen. 1:31).

Sometime after creation was completed, Lucifer, perhaps the highest angel, became proud of his great intelligence and beauty. He desired to become the king of the universe and to receive the praise and worship that belongs to God alone. Although a mere creature, he convinced himself that he could overthrow God's rule (1 Tim. 3:6; Ezek. 28:11-17; Isa. 14:12-14). In so doing, Lucifer rebelled against God's authority and refused to submit to God's rule. God, still in control, changed the rebel angel's name to Satan, which means **adversary,** and banished him from his former role. His authority was now limited to earth and the heavenly places around the earth (Ezek. 28:17; Eph 6:10-12).

In order to establish his rebel kingdom, Satan needed subjects and a place to rule. Therefore, he persuaded many angels to join him in his rebellion. He organized them and became their ruler (Matt. 12:24-46; Eph. 2:2; 6:11). Satan then tempted Adam to disobey God and rule his own life (Gen. 3:1-5). Adam did so and immediately came under Satan's dominion. He lost his ability to rule the earth for God because of sin, he was in rebellion toward God, the Ruler (Gen. 3:17-19; Rom. 5:12; 8:20-21). With man's fall into sin, Satan had succeeded in persuading **many** of God's angels and **all** of God's human servants to submit to his rule. His false rebel kingdom was now complete. He had authority and a place to rule and he exercised his authority over others.

Currently, every person enters Satan's kingdom simply by being born (Eph. 2:1-2). Although people are under and within God's eternal Kingdom, Satan directly rules all unsaved people. He is the "prince of the power of the air" and controls the whole world (1 John 5:19). His ongoing attempt to usurp God's sovereign rule takes place in human history on planet earth. The conflict of the ages is being fought all around us, and the two themes of authority and submission are at the heart of every conflict.

Pentecost gives a good description of the characteristics of Satan's kingdom:

> Because Satan's kingdom was instituted by lawlessness and rebellion, its chief characteristics are *lawlessness and rebellion* against the authority of God. All who are in Satan's kingdom oppose God, elevating themselves above Him who alone has the right to rule and be worshipped (2 Thess. 2:4).[3]

Six things happened with Adam sinned:

1B. Man died **spiritually** instantly, at the moment of disobedience (Gen. 2:16-17; Eph. 2:1-2). Do you remember when Adam hid from God?
Sin always alienates a person from a holy God.

2B. Man **eventually** died physically (Gen. 3:19; 5:5). When you read the first genealogy of Genesis, you read a phrase repeatedly, "and he died." Certainly, Adam lived physically a long time after he sinned, but he began to die and ever since, all men have died except for two supernatural

---

3. Pentecost, 25

interventions by God (Enoch and Elijah).

    3B. Man lost his ability to effectively **govern the earth** (Gen. 3:17-19; Heb. 2:5-8). Clearly, Adam had some control over the earth, but now, thorns and weeds grew. Others would be hard to work with. Adam himself would be plagued by sinful desires and tendencies making effective governance even more difficult.

    4B. Man's **environment** suffered the effects of his failure (Gen. 3:17-18; Rom. 8:19-22). Now thorns and thistles would be abundant and growing food would become harder. Mankind had been given work before the fall, now it would be much more difficult because of the consequences of the fall.

    5B. Man was transferred out of God's Kingdom and into **Satan's kingdom** (Col. 1:13; Acts 26:18). At birth, every person since the fall, apart from Jesus (His conception without human father enabled this) has been born a sinner, alienated from God, and a citizen of Satan's false kingdom.

    6B. Earth's government changed from a theocracy to a **Satanocracy** (Lk. 4:5-6; John 12:31; 1 John 5:19).

Now there are two opposing kingdoms. Satan works to destroy God's rule while God quietly works to restore His global kingdom. To demonstrate His sovereign authority and to **restore** His rule, God must provide salvation to rescue man from the satanic spiritual kingdom in which he is born. If His kingdom is to be a reality, God must also defeat Satan, destroy his false kingdom and restore his own theocracy on earth. God must reverse the six events that man's sin caused, and he must do so on this earth. God acts to restore His kingdom when:

1B. He makes humans **spiritually alive** through new birth (John 3:1-16; Titus 3:3-8). God, through Jesus' sacrifice and the individual response of faith by the sinner, makes people born dead spiritually alive instantly. They now have His life and are no longer alienated from God. Spiritual death is a separation from God, and therefore spiritual life includes a spiritual union with God.

2B. He abolishes physical death through **resurrection or rapture** (1 Tim. 1:10; 1 Thess. 4:13-18). Praise God that all who have died "in Christ" will be raised to new life. Additionally, the any moment possibility of a rapture provides hope that death may not even be a reality for the believer. The resurrected believers will receive a resurrected body while raptured living saints will be transformed to receive a glorified body.

3B. He will cause man to **govern** this earth as he originally intended (Heb. 2:5-9; Rev. 22:3-5). One day, mankind will rule, under the authority of king Jesus, the earth as it was created to do!

4B. He will **reverse** the effects of sin on this earth (Acts 3:21; Rom. 8:19-21; Rev. 22:1-5). In the future, the effects of sin and the curse upon creation will be completely reversed. Imagine a world where there is no more sin, no sickness, and no death!

5B. He **transfers believers** from Satan's kingdom to membership in His kingdom (Col. 1:13). At the moment of salvation, all believers are transferred from Satan's kingdom to Jesus. Our citizenship changes as we are adopted into the family of God (Phil. 3:20). We cease being subjects of Satan and immediately become subjects of the King!

6B. He will **dethrone Satan** and reestablish His earthly theocracy forever (Rev. 20-22). The last book of the Bible ends with Satan being incapacitated for the millennial kingdom, briefly released by God, and then forever defeated and cast into the lake of fire. Never again will he be able to rebel against the rule of the King.

When we come to the end of the Bible, we learn that God triumphs. The ultimate expression of God's kingdom in time is called the Millennium and will last for a thousand years. Jesus will be the King over all the earth then and Satan will be imprisoned (Rev. 20:1-6).

Following this 1,000-year Kingdom, Satan will be briefly released from his confinement. He will lead another earthly rebellion and attempt to become the sovereign (Rev. 20:7-10). God will defeat and punish forever Satan and the members of his rebellious kingdom (Rev. 20:11-15).

After this, God will make a new heaven and new earth where there will be no more **interruptions** of His righteous rule (1 Cor. 15:20-28; Rev. 21-22). Sin will be forever **gone**. Redeemed righteous men will serve God eternally and reign with Him forever (2 Pet. 3:10-13; Rev. 21:1-22:6). God's original intent for man, to rule as His representative on earth (Gen. 1:26-28), will then be eternally realized (Rev. 22:5).

CHAPTER 2 REVIEW/SUMMARY

1. The suggested theme of the Bible is "God's restoration of His Kingdom".

2. A legitimate kingdom must have three realities: 1) A ruler (king or queen); 2) Subjects and a realm (people and place) and 3) Exercise of authority (someone must rule, have authority).

3. When mankind sinned, as represented by Adam, many consequences followed. For God to restore His kingdom, those consequences must be reversed.

4. History will conclude with Jesus on His throne ruling over all He created and includes a new heaven and earth. Time, as we know it, will cease to be and our King will reign forever.

Chapter 3: DIFFERENT ASPECTS OF GOD'S KINGDOM

It is clear that God restoring His righteous earthly kingdom for His own glory is the thread that binds the Scripture together. It is also a thread that can be quite confusing! The Bible uses the term "kingdom" in various ways. Let's become acquainted with them.

1A. THE DISTINCTIONS OF GOD'S KINGDOM

Do some observation and see what you discover about God's kingdom. Below you will find a chart and a list of Scriptures. Read each passage and write its reference into the space that best summarizes what it teaches. Some passages may apply to more than one item. Read the passages carefully. You may also want to read the immediate context around each passage.

DISTINCTIONS IN GOD'S KINGDOM					
Time (When God rules)		**Scope** (Where God rules)		**Administration** (How God Rules)	
Eternal or Everlasting	Still to Come or In the Future	Universal Over All	Earth Alone	Directly Over All	Indirectly Over Earth

Read Daniel 2:35, 44, 45; 4:17, 35; 7:13, 14, 27. See also Psalms 103:19 and 135:6 along with Matthew 6:10 and Revelation 11:15. Place each reference in the appropriate category or categories above.

So, we discover three significant distinctions in the biblical concept of God's kingdom. Relative to **time**, God's kingdom is eternal but hasn't yet started. Regarding **scope**, it is universal yet on the earth alone. Finally, its **administration** is both directly by God and indirectly through a human agent on earth alone. Are these distinctions, contradictions, or something else?

2A. THE TWO PRIMARY ASPECTS OF THE KINGDOM

These distinctions aren't contradictions. Rather, they give a complete summary of God's kingdom. Like a coin with two sides, God's kingdom has two aspects.

1B. The Universal Kingdom

This is God's eternal rule over all places and creatures. All other forms of the kingdom are under and within the universal kingdom. Nothing happens in this kingdom outside of His permission and knowledge because He is Sovereign (1 Chron. 29:12; Ps. 145:13; Jer. 10:10). This is the broadest aspect of the kingdom. God rules directly (causes) and, at times, indirectly (allows), eternally, sovereignly and universally. Consider the following Scripture passages:

The LORD is King forever and ever;
Nations have perished from His land. Psalm 10:16

The LORD sat *as King* at the flood;
Yes, the LORD sits as King forever. Psalm 29:10

Yet God is my king from of old,
Who works deeds of deliverance in the midst of the earth. Psalm 74:12

Your kingdom is an everlasting kingdom,
And Your dominion *endures* throughout all generations. Psalm 145:13

But the LORD is the true God;
He is the living God and the everlasting King.
At His wrath the earth quakes,
And the nations cannot endure His indignation. Jeremiah 10:10

…that you be driven away from mankind and your dwelling place be with the beasts of the field, and you be given grass to eat like cattle and be drenched with the dew of heaven; and seven periods of time will pass over you, until you recognize that the Most High is ruler over the realm of mankind and bestows it on whomever He wishes. Daniel 4:25

For additional study, consider Psalm 90:1-6; 103:19-22; 148:1-14; Lamentations 5:19; Daniel 6:26 and Amos 9:2.

2B. The Millennial Kingdom

As previously stated, a theocracy is a form of government in which a human representative administers God's rule. In Eden, God's theocracy was through Adam over the earth. When Adam sinned, that theocracy became a Satanocracy (don't look the word up in a dictionary; a friend of mine coined it!). However, God intends to restore His theocracy in the future. It will be over all the earth, through a human administrator and is yet future (Ps. 2; Is. 9:6-7; 11:1-10; 65:17-25).

That time will be in the future Millennium when the Great King, the Lord Jesus, rules all the earth. Lasting a thousand years, this theocracy is yet future (Rev 20:1-6). Jesus will reign from Jerusalem over all the earth and Israel will have a key global role.

This is the reason so many Old Testament references look ahead to that coming period.

The Millennium will conclude by merging into the Eternal Kingdom. Eternal Kingdom is a term used only to distinguish between it and Millennial Kingdom. It is a biblical concept though not a term found in the Bible. Some writers use the term "new kingdom" because it occurs within a new heaven and earth (Isa. 65:17; Rev. 21). It is the last step in God restoring His righteous rule on earth. It will include all creation and will last forever on the new earth. (Rev. 21:5). This aspect of the kingdom is also mentioned in 1 Cor. 15:23-28. When Jesus starts to rule in the millennial kingdom there will be no end to His rule (Isa. 9:6,7) but there will be a rebellion, a restoration of heaven and earth, and the complete removal of the curse as the eternal kingdom begins.

To summarize: when the Bible describes God's Kingdom it usually speaks to one of two basic aspects. One is God's direct, absolute ownership and rule of all things, His universal kingdom. The other is God's delegated, still to come earthly kingdom. What about the period between the original theocracy and the realization of the one yet to come?

3A. THE OUTWORKING OF GOD'S RULE

Different aspects of God's rule before the coming Millennium become clear as Scripture progressively unfolds. We must distinguish between these to read the Bible accurately. There are three aspects of God's Kingdom program to recognize.

1B. The **spiritual** kingdom

Within the universal kingdom is God's rule over all whom the Holy Spirit makes spiritually alive by grace through faith (John 3:1-10; Titus 3:3-7). Everyone, from Adam until the end of the age, who believes God's promise for life is graciously **translated** out of the kingdom of darkness into God's spiritual kingdom. Colossians 1:13 states, *"For He rescued us from the domain of darkness and transferred us to the kingdom of His beloved Son."*

This is one of the major reasons why the New Testament makes such a point about the concept of adoption. Those who believe Jesus' promise for everlasting life are adopted by God, made sons and daughters in His eternal family (cf. Rom. 8:15, 23; 9:4; Gal. 4:5; Eph. 1:5).

Put another way, the spiritual kingdom includes all believers of human history. This facet of the kingdom began at Adam's conversion and will run throughout human history. The church is part of the spiritual kingdom. Sometimes the Bible describes the spiritual kingdom as the "kingdom of heaven" and other times the "kingdom of God."

2B. The **national** kingdom

This is God's rule over the nation Israel (Exod. 19:1-6). This was established at Sinai when Israel entered a covenant relationship with God and agreed to keep his law. God administered his rule over Israel through the judges, kings and prophets. The national kingdom was destroyed when Babylon carried Judah away into captivity but will be renewed in the Millennium. This is based upon the fact that the northern kingdom of Israel, had been defeated and deported by the Assyrians in 722 B.C. and the southern kingdom, Judah, by Babylon (605-586 BC) leaving no kingdom left in the land of promise.

In the future, David will be resurrected and be Prince of Israel.

And I, the LORD, will be their God, and My servant David will be prince among them; I the LORD have spoken. Ezekiel 34:24

My servant David will be king over them, and they will all have one shepherd; and they will walk in My ordinances and keep My statutes and observe them. Ezekiel 37:24

3B. The **interim** kingdom

Perhaps you've been a part of a church where the pastor resigned or retired. Often the church is not ready to hire a new pastor, so they appoint what is often called an interim pastor. The interim is viewed as the temporary leader between the last "official" leader and the next one to be hired. The interim kingdom occurs between the offer of the kingdom and its becoming a reality.

In Matthew 13, Jesus taught "the mysteries of the kingdom." A "mystery" is a truth not revealed in the Old Testament but now **made known** in the New Testament. What Jesus taught about the kingdom in Matthew 13 was not in the Old Testament. These mysteries describe an interim form of the kingdom. It began with Jesus' rejection by the nation Israel (Matt. 12:15-ff) and will continue until their acceptance of Him as Messiah at His return just before He establishes the Millennial Kingdom (Zech. 9:9; 12:10). Put another way, the interim kingdom began roughly in 30 A.D., at Jesus' rejection by Israel's leaders, and will continue until His second coming to be King.

It includes all living people, the church, Satan and his hosts (the fallen angels). Do you remember Jesus' parable about the wheat and tares (Matt. 13:24-30)? Both the wheat and the tares grew side by side until the end of the age. During the interim between Jesus' offer of a kingdom and Israel's acceptance of Him as her King, Satan will be active, and unbelievers will often be among believers in life. Sometimes the gospels refer to it as the "kingdom of heaven" and other times as the "kingdom of God." It will be followed by the Millennium.

With so many aspects of the kingdom, things can get quite confusing. Remember though that a diamond is attractive because it has so many facets carved into one stone. That is the way it is with God's kingdom once you start to grasp it. Perhaps the chart that follows will help you picture the various uses of "kingdom."

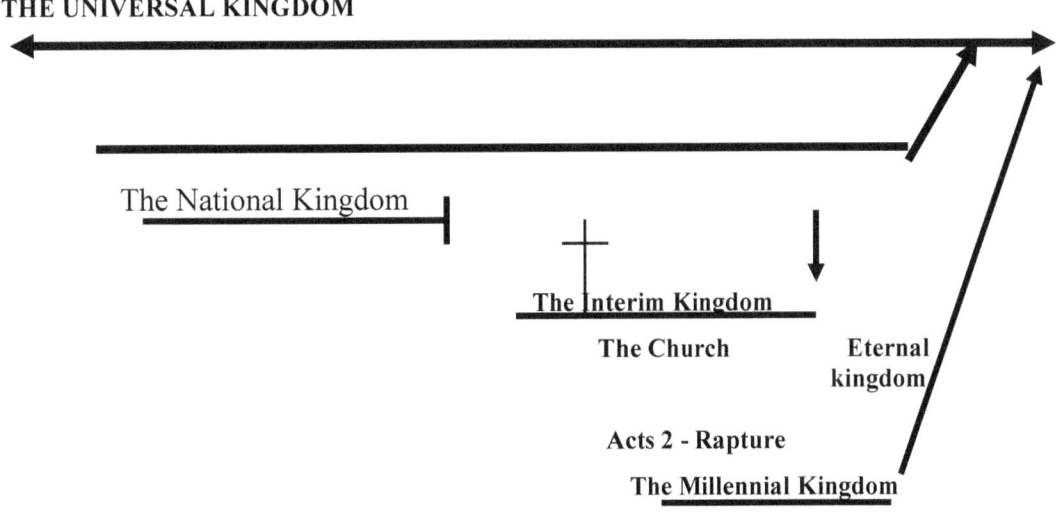

From start to finish, the Bible is about God acting to restore His earthly Kingdom and vindicate His sovereignty. The rest of this book will deal with the progressive revelation concerning how God acts to restore His righteous earthly rule.

CHAPTER 3 REVIEW/SUMMARY

1. There are two primary aspects of God's kingdom:

A.   The universal kingdom refers to God's sovereign rule over all people in all places at all times.

B.   The millennial kingdom refers to God's future personal rule over all the earth through His anointed one, Jesus Christ.

2. The outworking of God's rule:

A.   The spiritual kingdom includes all believers of all the ages. Every person who has ever believed God's promise for life is included in the spiritual kingdom.

B. The national kingdom is God's rule over the nation of Israel. It began at Sinai continued until the Babylonian captivity. It ended when Israel ceased to have her own kings rule over them.

C. The interim kingdom was/is the time between Jesus' rejection by Israel as her king until her acceptance of Him as her king as His second coming. It includes all people and all angels during that time frame.

Chapter 4: PEOPLE, PROMISES and PERIODS

Since God is working to restore his kingdom on earth, He must work through people. Let's overview what the Scripture teaches about how He does this. Three key areas help us understand God's progressive revelation about His kingdom.

1A. THE PEOPLE WITH WHOM GOD WORKS

One passage in the New Testament summarizes how God views and relates to humanity. The text is 1 Corinthians 10:32, "Give no offense either to Jews or to Greeks or to the church of God."

From God's perspective, every person is in one of three categories.

> 1B. **Jews** are physical descendants of Abraham **through Isaac and Jacob**. Abraham had many descendants (Ishmael and the sons of Keturah- see Genesis 25:1, 2) but the Bible does not declare them to be Jewish. Esau, Abraham's grandson, and his descendants are further examples of this concept. Therefore, the Bible often uses the phrase, "the God of Abraham, Isaac and Jacob" or similar words. Scripture also refers to them as Israel and as God's chosen people. The Jewish people are recipients of God's special grace and the people through whom the King was promised to come (Rom. 9:3-5).
>
> 2B. **Greeks / Gentiles:** These are non-Jewish people groups. Sometimes the Bible refers to them as "the nations." Gentiles were not given any spiritual privileges as was Israel. Indeed, until Christ

came, they had no hope (Eph. 3:1-7). This group includes everyone who is not Jewish, and every other ethnic group on planet earth.

3B. The **Church**: Before the day of Pentecost (Acts 2), there was no church. Every person was either a Jew or a Gentile. He was either a believing or a lost Jew or Gentile. However, God created a new body at Pentecost that came to be called the church. The church consists of all believers in Christ from Pentecost until the rapture. In this age, when people believe in Jesus, God no longer sees them as a Jew or a Gentile, but as part of the church. One uniqueness of the church is that, though saved the same way a saint from previous times was, everyone who is part of the church has been baptized by the Holy Spirit into Christ's body and permanently indwelt by the Spirit (1 Cor. 12:13; Rom. 8:9).

When reading God's Word, wise is the person who asks, "What people group was this passage addressed to?" If it was addressed to another group, it might not apply to the reader, just as a law written to Canadians in the 1920's probably does not apply to you as a citizen of the United States.

As God works in and through each people group, He does so in various ways and times. These ways and times are called covenants and dispensations in the Bible. Covenants and dispensations are big words! They are also keys to understanding God's progressive revelation. They are like stitches that bind the story together or like the border pieces of a jigsaw puzzle that enable you to complete the picture. Let's become familiar with both.

2A. THE PROMISES THROUGH WHICH GOD WORKS - COVENANT

In our study, we will overview the major theological covenants of Scripture. There are other biblical covenants, but they are not our subjects in this class.

We call them **theological** covenants because God makes them to bring about His purposes. The theological covenants reveal **how** God relates to His subjects as He acts to restore His rule. They also tell **what** man's responsibilities are.

1B. A definition of covenant:

A covenant is a binding agreement between two or more people/parties concerning shared responsibilities and privileges A covenant, once ratified, cannot be changed in any way, including the parties involved, the covenant conditions or the covenant provisions.

Galatians 3:15 states this truth, *"Brethren, I speak in terms of human relations: even though it is only a man's covenant, yet when it has been ratified, no one sets it aside or adds conditions to it"*.

God makes two types of covenants with men.

    1C. **Unconditional** Covenants:

God grants some benefit to another party with no conditions upon the recipient. It must be noted however that to enjoy the provisions of the covenant some action is required. An illustration would be the covenant of marriage is to be entered unconditionally. But to truly and fully be enjoyed, each party should relate to his/her spouse in a loving way. It is important to note that the term "unconditional" is not used in the text of scripture. How then does one know if the covenant is unconditional? It is by the language of the covenant.

Unconditional covenants use language such as "I will..." But they do not have language such as, "I will, IF you...."

2C. **Conditional** Covenants:

God grants some benefit to another party if / when they fulfill the conditions expressed in the covenant. As noted, this type of covenant includes statements such as, "...if you will... then I will...."

2B. The Theological covenants.

These theological covenants are the "mountain peaks" of God's progressive revelation – later revelation flows from and about them. The following chart summarizes those we will study as we work our way through God's progressive revelation. We are not going to cover all of them – just the six key covenants.

THEOLOGICAL COVENANTS		
NAME	TYPE	PRIMARY TEXT
Adamic	Conditional	Gen. 1:26-28
Abrahamic	Unconditional	Gen. 12:1-3; 15:1-21
Mosaic	Conditional	Exod. 19:1-8
Land/Palestinian	Unconditional	Deut. 28-30
Davidic	Unconditional	2 Sam. 7:10-16
New	Unconditional	Jer. 31:31-40; Matt. 26:26-30

3B. The Application of the Covenants

    1C. The theological covenants contain material that applies to **specific individuals**, groups or nations. This is called the **limited application**. As an example, in the Abrahamic Covenant, God promised to make Abraham's name great. It is a misapplication of Scripture to claim that promise for one's self or anyone else. Put another way, some, most, or all of the promises of a covenant might not apply to you.

    2C. At the same time, some covenants pertain to **all men** in all times and places. This is called **universal application**. Certain features of a covenant are given to a broader group of people. For example, God promised to make Israel into a great nation as part of the Abrahamic Covenant. This is something He did when He grew Israel into millions of people and gave them her land of promise. He also promised to bless all the peoples of the earth. The apostle Paul applied that to the church in Galatians 3:8. That is a universal application. The New Testament usually leaves no doubt as to what is and is not binding on us today. Some covenants also have been fulfilled while others await some future fulfillment.

    3C. Finally, all the covenants will find their ultimate fulfillment in the person of Jesus Christ, God's soon coming King (2 Cor. 1:20). When He reigns in His Millennial Kingdom, all covenants will be fulfilled. This is the **theocratic application.**

3A. THE PERIODS IN WHICH GOD WORKS – DISPENSATIONS

1B. A Definition

The word "dispensation" comes from the Greek word "oikonomia," which means **stewardship** or **household management**. See Luke 16:2, 3, 4; 1 Cor. 9:17; Eph. 1:10; 3:2, 9; Gal. 3:19; 1 Tim. 1:4. A dispensation is a distinct period of human responsibility in the outworking of God's purpose. As an example, a business owner might delegate the oversight of one unit of his business to a manager while he is gone. He might declare that he will review inventory and profits upon his return in six months. In those six months, the manager is responsible to do the will of the owner.

Dispensations present history as a **household** overseen by God. In His household, God delegates to his **covenant subjects** certain responsibilities as managers of His kingdom purpose. In each age, God puts his covenant subjects under a responsibility; they fail and God judges. Thus, dispensations have three aspects: (1) **responsibility** (2) **failure** and (3) **judgment / discipline**.

Through history, God exercises His rule through different means at different times. The Bible refers to these times of God's rule as ***dispensations***. A dispensation is merely a period of time, an era. The word technically means, "household management." It is how God manages/administers/rules His "household"/creation. The verses below detail more about this concept. Suffice it to say there are two dispensation/periods of time that dominate most of the pages of the Bible. The **Law** was given to Israel in Exodus 19 and continues through the New Testament Gospels. Remember when Jesus said he was about to institute a new covenant and with it a new dispensation? The second major dispensation is the **Church Dispensation** (sometimes referred to as "the dispensation of grace"). It began at Pentecost

(Acts 2) and essentially runs through most of the rest of the New Testament. Sometimes a text will be in one dispensation but will speak of future or past dispensations. Accurate interpretation and application demand that we understand the dispensational context of every text we study. Notice the following verses:

- "…with a view to an ***administration*** suitable to the fullness of the times, *that is*, the summing up of all things in Christ, things in the heavens and things on the earth. In Him" (Eph. 1:10 – The King James Version of the Bible uses the word, "dispensation" here).

- "…if indeed you have heard of the ***stewardship*** of God's grace which was given to me for you and to bring to light what is the ***administration*** of the mystery which for ages has been hidden in God who created all things." (Eph. 3:2, 9; once again the KJV uses the term "dispensation" here.).

- "Why the ***Law*** then? It was ***added*** because of transgressions, having been ordained through angels by the agency of a mediator, until the seed would come to whom the promise had been made" (Gal 3:19).

Two illustrations of this concept from the history of the United States might be helpful. Considering the United States Constitution might be useful in giving clarity to the subject. The eighteenth amendment to the U.S. Constitution was passed in 1920 and prohibited the sale, distribution, and consumption of all alcoholic beverages in the United States (known as Prohibition). Later in 1933, the twenty-first amendment was passed which overturned the previous prohibition on alcohol. These two amendments represent two "dispensations", or periods, in U.S. history. During one period (dispensation) it was illegal to sell, possess, consume, or purchase alcohol. During the second, it was legally permissible.

Another historical reality helps illustrate this principle. In the United States in the 1960's, the legal voting age was twenty-one years of age. During the Vietnam War era, many young men and women protested, stating the U.S. government considered them adults by sending them to war but would not let them vote. In 1971, the 26th amendment was passed giving 18-year-old citizens the right to register to vote. Prior to 1971 it was illegal for all citizens of the United States under the age of twenty-one to vote but legal and even encouraged after that time for those who were eighteen years old or older and who were citizens and were registered to vote.

Both historical events demonstrate the principle of dispensations. They are merely an era, or a time period. What occurs during that period? We often speak of a president's time in office as his administration. During the four, or perhaps eight years he was in office how did he manage the country?

On a personal level, every person's life has different dispensations. Each of us had a time when we were confined, very comfortably, in our mother's womb. Then we had childhood. Most of us received a driver's license (freedom!) at age sixteen. Many got married in their twenties and many have children in their 20's and 30's. These are distinct periods in a person life and to fail to recognize them would be a failure to understand life (eighteen-year old adults don't still take naps or go to bed at 8:00 PM and three-year old toddlers can't legally drive a car).

A failure to employ a literal hermeneutic (interpretive principles for Bible study) will result in an aversion to the concept of dispensations and great confusion in interpretation. For example, the law commanded people to only wear clothing that was of one kind of material – it had to be 100% cotton or 100% wool, with no mixture allowed (Lev. 19:19; Deut. 22:11). Additionally, in Matthew 10:5, 6, Jesus commanded His disciples to go ONLY to those who were lost Jews and to NOT go to the Gentiles or Samaritans. Yet in Matthew

28:18-20 and Acts 1:8 He sent them to proclaim the message of salvation to the whole world, including Samaritans and Gentiles.

Covenants reveal **how** God relates to His subjects as He acts to restore His rule. They also tell **what** man's responsibilities are. Dispensations deal with man's **response over time** to that administration.

For example, in North Carolina, there are covenants (laws) and periods (dispensations) that regulate the privilege of driving a motor vehicle. When a resident of North Carolina reaches the age of fifteen years, she can get a driver's permit but with several stipulations, including but not limited to the following – successfully complete a Driver's Education course beforehand; have parent or guardian present in the front seat of the vehicle while operating it, and to drive only certain hours each day. The permit must be obtained at least one year before a driver's license can be obtained (the year is equivalent to a dispensation). When that period of time is over, the young lady may attempt to pass a driving test in order to obtain a provisional driver's license. If she passes, the rules change (covenant). She no longer needs a parent or guardian with her but must still follow some carefully prescribed rules.

I have many cousins who grew up in a distant state (Iowa) while I grew up in Oklahoma. They were under some very different driver's license regulations, because they were part of a different people group. They were Iowans, while I was an Oklahoman. Different groups of people often operate under differing rules.

2B. The Number of Dispensations

Surveying the New Testament, we find that God has progressively revealed Himself in at least four distinct periods / ages / dispensations in which He ruled differently. You should note that some features from one dispensation are often carried into later ones; thus, elements from earlier periods continue in subsequent dispensations. Each has a different covenant as its basis. The chart below shows this.

*Note that classic dispensationalism has seven dispensations, while we will only dwell on four. We will prove the four scripturally. The three we skip are commonly called, Innocence, Conscience, and Human Government. They reflect the truths found in Genesis 1-11, that mankind was created in Innocence, having no sin nature but possessing the ability to choose to obey or disobey God. This age lasted an indeterminate length of time, but it is covered in Genesis 13. The dispensation of Conscience began as soon as Adam and Eve sinned and knew what it meant to sin and not obey God. Now they had an internal "compass" to either approve or condemn their actions, thoughts, and motives. This era began in Genesis 3 and continued until Genesis 8. Mankind did not live up to the standards it knew to be right and became more and more evil. After God sent the Flood to destroy the earth and begin anew with righteous Noah, God instituted what we know as Human Government. In Genesis 9 God gave mankind (government) and not individuals, the authority to punish sin. When we get to Genesis 12, we see much more detail about the new era that will launch yet another dispensation. If the Scriptures are interpreted at face value, a student of the Bible will recognize multiple dispensations.

THE DISPENSATIONS				
NAME	COVENANT	TEXT	DESCRIPTION	PRIMARY TEXT
Promise	Adamic	Gen. 12 – Exod. 18	All mankind from Adam to Mt. Sinai	Gen. 1:28-3:6
Law	Mosaic	Exod. 19- Acts 1	The national life of Israel to Christ's death	Exod. 19:1; Rom. 10:4
Church	New	Acts 2 – Rev.19	The church from Pentecost to the Rapture	1 Cor. 11:23-26
Millennium / Kingdom	Abrahamic	Rev. 20- 22	The 1,000-year reign of Christ on earth	Gen. 12:1-3

Ephesians mentions three dispensations. Ephesians 1:10 states that God planned a future stewardship or dispensation in which Christ will ultimately head up all things. He describes this future dispensation as "the fullness of the times" or "the summing up of all things in Christ." That has not yet happened; it is a **future** dispensation which we will call the **kingdom**. It will be a time when Jesus reigns on earth and is the central figure in all world affairs (e.g., "the summing up of all things in Christ").

In Ephesians 3:2,9, Paul refers to a **second** stewardship or dispensation. It was previously unrevealed but is now made known (in the New Testament era) by God through Paul. It is the **present** age, in which Gentiles are fellow heirs with Jews (v. 6). This dual privilege did not occur until Acts 2; hence, Paul sees the **church** age as a different dispensation. In so doing, he contrasts it with the **previous** age, which was under law. So, Paul refers to three dispensations in Ephesians 1 and 3. **The past age is the law, the present is the church age (often referred to as the dispensation of grace), and the future dispensation is the Millennium.**

Galatians 3:19-25 hints at the fourth dispensation. The Law was "added" which means there was an age already in force when the law was given to Israel through Moses at Mount Sinai (Exod. 19, 20). Romans 5:12-14 refers to that period before the Law, which we call the **Promise** era. It ran from Abraham to Mt. Sinai (Genesis 12 – Exodus 18).

4A. SALVATION THROUGH THE AGES

Some are confused about how people were saved in other dispensations. Was it by bringing the correct sacrifice? Keeping the law? Has God's method of salvation changed along with the covenants and dispensations?

NO! God has always saved man by His grace through faith in His promise. God always initiates and provides for salvation – this is grace. God always states something to be believed or rejected – a promise. Mankind always chooses to accept or reject God's provision – this is faith. As we will see, throughout human history the only way anyone was ever declared righteous (justified) was by God's grace through faith in His promise. God's grace saves us; our faith in His promise is simply the channel through which His grace is received.

What has changed consistently is revelation concerning the **object** of faith – what man is to trust. It is not our sincerity or the amount of our faith that makes faith effective. It is the object of faith – what we trust – that makes faith effective.

Because God **revealed Himself progressively**, the content of His promises was also revealed step by step. For instance, Adam knew nothing of the person, life, crucifixion, or resurrection of Jesus Christ. Yet, he was saved by grace through faith! In what did he put his faith? He believed God's **promise** that he would provide a seed of the woman to crush the serpent's head (Gen. 3:15). When Adam and Eve trusted God's promise, God justified them and began to direct them. That is salvation: God graciously initiated the process and made a promise; Adam believed it and God faithfully responded. Only later was it revealed that the seed of the woman would be Jewish, and a direct descendant of Abraham (Genesis 12:3). Still later, that He would be born of the tribe of Judah (Gen. 49:10-12); born of a virgin (Isa. 7:14); and born in Bethlehem (Micah 5:2). Then much later that He would die on a cross and conquer the grave through resurrection (1 Cor. 15:3, 4).

So, the bottom line is that, in all dispensations, God always saves by <u>His grace through our faith in His promise</u>. God's promise is that if you believe on the Lord Jesus Christ, you will be saved. His sinless life provides the perfect righteousness God requires of you. His death satisfies God's wrath against your sin, because Jesus died as your substitute. Finally, God is so pleased with who Jesus is and what He did that He raised Jesus from the dead. His resurrection proves He is Savior King and that God is satisfied with His work. You must trust Jesus to receive His righteousness in exchange for your sin and His life in return for your death. Have you been saved? To get saved you don't need to be baptized, change your behavior, confess, or turn over a new leaf. You do need to trust Jesus Christ.

Have you trusted in Jesus Christ? If you haven't, you can do so right now, wherever you are. If you do, tell Him that you believe He is your SaviorKing and thank Him for your forgiveness. Tell a friend, relative or someone else that you have done so – they will want to celebrate with you. If you have trusted Jesus sometime previously, stop right now and thank Him for being the object of your faith, and thank God for His grace to you!

We have studied an incredible amount in these first four chapters. You have done well staying with it and grasping new ideas. The chart below puts together all we've discussed of God's program of restoring His rule. Notice the universal kingdom, Satan's false kingdom and the various dispensations throughout human history, through which God's spiritual kingdom always runs.

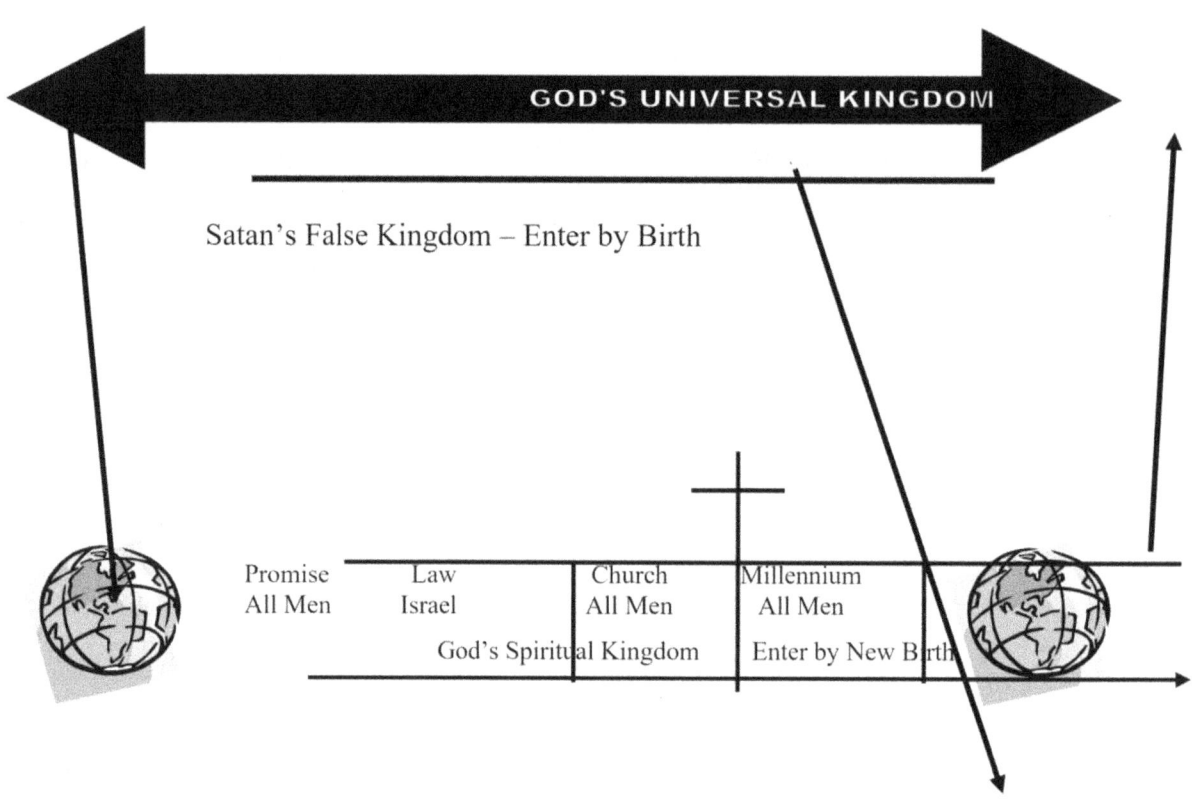

CHAPTER 4 REVIEW/SUMMARY

1. The people with whom God works are: Jews (descendants of Abraham through Isaac and Jacob), Gentiles (all non-Jews) and the church (all saved people from the day of Pentecost/Acts 2 until the rapture no matter what nation or tribe they are from), see 1 Corinthians 10:32.

2. A covenant is a binding agreement between two or more parties. It details the responsibilities of the person(s) who enter the covenant.

3. There are two types of covenants, conditional and unconditional. Even in unconditional covenants, certain responsibilities must be undertaken to fully enjoy the provisions of the covenant.

4. In applying the covenants, there may be personal application, national application, and universal application. Context and specific language of the covenant will reveal which one(s) are appropriate.

5. A dispensation is an age/era during which God administers His "household" in a specific way. There are at least four dispensations that cover most of the Bible (Promise, Law, Grace/Church, and Kingdom); See Ephesians 1:10; 3:2,9; Galatians 3:19-25.

Chapter 5: FROM EDEN TO UR

4000+/- BC – 2150 BC

Genesis 1-11

This chapter focuses on God's earliest acts related to His kingdom restoration work. We will only hit the **high points** as there is so much material in these passages. It is somewhat interesting that the first eleven chapters of Genesis cover about two thousand years, while the remainder of all the Old Testament and New Testament cover only slightly more than that.

1A. FROM PARADISE TO THE FLOOD (Gen 1:1-8:19)

God placed Adam on earth as His theocratic ruler (one placed in a position of authority directly by God to administer God's rule). Reflecting God's image, Adam was like God in his ability to rule (Gen. 1:26-28). Adam was not a sinner when God created him, though he had the capacity to sin because God gave him the ability to choose contrary to his nature. Adam and Eve's innocence allowed for remarkable fellowship with God and one another in the garden.

God outlined his will for Adam and his descendants. He was responsible for four basic things:

- Be **fruitful**, multiply and fill the earth (Gen. 1:28).

- **Rule** the earth and the animals (Gen. 1:28).

- **Care** for the Garden in Eden (Gen. 2:15).

- Attain the knowledge of good by **obedience** (Gen. 2:17).

For an indefinite time after creation, all was very good under God's rule (1:31). Evidently, Satan rebelled sometime after Genesis 1:31 and corrupted God's universal kingdom. Satan persuaded Adam to join him in his revolt against God. Instead of ruling the serpent and Eve, Adam submitted to her after she submitted to Satan (Gen. 3:1-6,17). Adam, might have stood beside Eve during the temptation, but definitely ate from the tree rather than abstaining (Gen. 3:6 cf. 1 John 2:16). Now, the original couple knew good and evil by experience (Gen. 3:7). Spiritual death immediately followed and physical death quickly followed (Gen. 2:17; Rom. 5:12).

Because God's earthly representatives had **defected**, God's theocracy was lost from planet earth – His appointed rulers, Adam and Eve, had rebelled against Him. Satan, through his rebellion toward God and his temptation of mankind, usurped both the right to rule and the realm to rule over. Eden was polluted, but God did not abandon His creation or plan. Now that Satan had conquered all humans, God responded with grace and judgment.

God promised Satan that the woman's seed would defeat him in the coming spiritual conflict (Gen. 3:15). God sentenced woman to sorrow and pain, and Adam to exhausting and frustrating labor (Gen. 3:16-19). God also cursed the earth for Adam's sake. This curse was a measure of grace in that it enabled Adam to still rule the earth to some degree (Gen. 3:17-19; Rom. 8:19-21).

Adam and Eve demonstrated their faith as Adam immediately resumed headship over the woman and named her Eve, which means **living**. In this name, Adam anticipated God keeping His promise of the coming victory over Satan.

Since the first Adam lost God's theocracy, the last Adam (1 Cor. 15:45) must regain it on earth. Jesus, as the last Adam, will do three things to regain His theocracy.

- He will **defeat Satan**, remove his followers, and imprison him (Heb. 2:14; Rev. 6-19, 20). All rebellion against the King must be stopped for Him to have true dominion.

- He will **reign** over all the earth (Isa. 9:6,7; Rev. 20:1-6). His rule will extend from the north pole to the south pole and all the way from east to west.

- He will **rule creation** and remove the curse (Matt. 19:28; Acts 3:1921). He will not merely rule people, but also all He created.

After their exile from the garden, Adam and Eve were to live by their knowledge of good and evil (what we call conscience; Gen. 3:22; Rom. 2:14-15) and by the promises and directives God gave (3:14-19 and 4:1-7). Their descendants demonstrate the presence of the **two kingdoms in conflict**. Cain, who slew righteous Abel, Lamech who violated God's material and moral laws and the corrupt sons of God all demonstrate their allegiance to Satan's kingdom of darkness (Gen. 4-8). Meanwhile, a few bright lights shone in the darkness. Righteous Abel, Seth, Lamech (a different one than previously mentioned), Noah, and Enoch are the ones named who trusted God's promises and walked with Him. Although God's kingdom people were in the minority, they were present. However, almost the entire human race became corrupt as Satan attempted to prevent the promised seed from coming (Gen. 3:15; 6:1-8).

2A. AFTER THE FLOOD TO ABRAHAM (Gen 8:20-12:3)

In righteousness God determined to judge the world with a **worldwide** flood. Before the flood, God promised Noah He would "establish his covenant" with him (Gen 6:17-18). God would continue His purpose of ruling earth through righteous men after He removed the wicked ones from earth. God faithfully kept His word to Noah.

The Flood destroyed all of mankind except for Noah and his family (Gen. 6:9-8:12; cf. 2 Peter 2:4,5; Jude 6,7). God then made an eternal covenant with Noah in Genesis 8:13-9:17, and its sign was a rainbow. Human history began anew with a single family who trusted Him. You never know how great an impact one righteous life can have! Note also that God initiated the covenant as Noah was worshipping God (Gen. 8:20).

Did God change His plans for humanity? Absolutely not! He reiterated man's purpose to fill the earth to both Noah (Gen. 9:2) and his descendants (Gen. 9:8-10).

> [8]The fear of you and the terror of you will be on every beast of the earth and on every bird of the sky; with everything that creeps on the ground, and all the fish of the sea, into your hand they are given. Then God spoke to Noah and to his sons with him, saying, [9] "Now behold, I Myself do establish My covenant with you, and with your descendants after you; [10] and with every living creature that is with you, the birds, the cattle, and every beast of the earth with you; of all that comes out of the ark, even every beast of the earth.

He also enabled them to exercise some **dominion** over the animals, and instituted **government** as the means to exercise His authority. Mankind was now to promote good and punish evil, particularly murder, through a more centralized form. Despite man's sinfulness, God will fulfill His purpose to have man reign on earth. He spells this out in the Noahic Covenant.

The chart below summarizes it:

THE NOAHIC COVENANT		
Parties: All men	**Type:** Unconditional	**Text:** Gen. 8:15-9:17
How God Related to Man		**What Man Was to Do**
Provides for the increase of the race (9:1) Provides fear of man in animals (9:2) Provides food, including meat (9:3-4) Protects the sanctity of life via government (9:3) Promised to never destroy the race with a flood (9:11)		**Populate** the earth (9:1,11) Avoid eating **lifeblood** (9:4) Protect human life via **government** (9:5-6)
Universal Application		
All the above		
Theocratic Application		
Christ will govern the earth perfectly in the future (Isa. 9:6-7)		

From Noah's family, the conflict between the kingdoms of light and darkness erupted again. Ham, Noah's son, sinned in some way against his father and the Lord. As the theocratic ruler, Noah cursed Canaan, Ham's son. Ham became the first of a line of people through whom Satan's false kingdom would develop. His spiritual darkness grew even darker in his descendants. Ham means the "**hot one**." To Ham was born Cush, which means "**blackened one**," and Cush fathered Nimrod, which means "**rebellion**." These names describe the lack of spiritual receptivity of those individuals named.

The Satanic attacks continued when Nimrod, an early governmental leader, led a rebellion against God. Genesis 10:9 describes him as a "mighty hunter **against** the Lord." (Note: some translations translate the phrase "a mighty hunter **before** the Lord". The Hebrew language and context support the idea of "against," or "in the face" rebel). He opposed God's will and founded several cities, chief of which was Babylon (10:10). From this point forward in Scripture, Babylon, is the location of the first organized global rebellion against God and is frequently the earthly center of satanic opposition to God's rule. It often symbolizes a works-based system of self-sufficient religion.

God had commanded mankind to scatter and fill the earth (Gen. 9:1,7). Nimrod led the peoples to unite politically and religiously against God (Gen. 10:8-12; 11:1-4). Satan now used human government, instituted by God to express His rule, against God, and to challenge His rule. In sovereign power, God acted to **confound** the rebellion and **scatter** the nations, thus demonstrating His authority (Gen. 11:7-9). God sovereignly did three things to advance His purpose to restore his rule on earth. First, He **overthrew** the earthly government that opposed His will (Gen. 11:1-9). Second, God **confused** man's speech and created the nations as He scattered them according to their languages (Gen. 11:5-9). Third, and perhaps most importantly, He promised to **bless all nations** through a descendant of Shem (Gen. 12:3). This promise is part of the Abrahamic Covenant. It is so important we will devote an entire chapter to it.

To this point in the Scripture narrative, God's kingdom purpose *seems* to have fallen on hard times. Satan, in the Garden, usurped His original rule. Then Satan attempted to corrupt the entire race so the promised seed could not be born (Gen. 3:15). After universal judgment through the flood, God began again. This time Satan inspired man's rebellion through God's appointed means of rule, **government**. Therefore, God scattered man and created the nations. From these nations, God selected another avenue to fulfill his purpose – Abraham and his seed.

A chart will help to summarize the progressive revelation in the first eleven chapters of Genesis.

DISPENSATION OF PROMISE					
Man's Responsibility	**God's Covenant**	**Man's Failure**	**God's Judgment**	**God's Gracious Revelation**	**Main Text**
Rule Earth	Adamic	Submit to Satan	Fall	Woman's Seed	Gen. 1-3
Look for Seed		Satanic corruption	Flood	Line of Shem	Gen. 4-9
Fill Earth	Noahic	Stayed together	Scattering	Universal blessing	Gen. 10-12

CHAPTER 5 REVIEW/SUMMARY

1. God delegated authority to humans (Adam and Eve) to rule over His creation. This is called a theocracy.

2. Sometime prior to Genesis 3 Satan rebelled against God and led many other angels to rebel (Isaiah 14 and Ezekiel 28). He tempted Adam and Eve to rebel, and they used their freedom of choice to do so. Satan now had a kingdom which included beings/people (some angels and all people), a realm (earth and surrounding atmosphere) and authority ("god of this world").

3. The early chapters of Genesis record the two kingdoms in conflict. Some people mentioned were godly, but most were not. Eventually God responded to the wickedness of man and destroyed the earth with a worldwide flood.

4. God established a covenant with Noah which included a sign (rainbow) and the beginning of human government (God's newly revealed means of regulating sin and promoting righteousness), Genesis 8:15-9:7.

5. Mankind continued to rebel against God, led by Nimrod (Genesis 10 & 11). God responded by confusing mankind by means of creating many languages and scattering mankind over the face of the earth (Genesis 11:5-9).

Chapter 6: FROM UR TO SINAI
(2150 – 1445 BC)
Genesis 11:10 – Exodus 18:27

The Bible is about God's intention to restore His rule over and on earth. After Adam sinned, God began this process. He did so by promising a ruler / redeemer and providing for a relationship with Himself through faith in His promise. Satan attempted to prevent the promised one from coming by corrupting the race, and men cooperated with him. Humanity became so corrupt that God destroyed all people except Noah's family. With this family, God made another covenant (the Noahic Covenant - with rainbow as a sign – Gen. 9) and reiterated His desire that men rule the earth. Ham, one of Noah's sons, sinned and was cursed. His descendants reflected that same sinful attitude and rebelled against God's Kingship. Led by Nimrod at Babylon, mankind determined to establish its own kingdom and own religion in opposition to God's rule. Therefore, God **scattered them**. Genesis 11: 9 states, *"Therefore its name was called Babel, because there the LORD confused the language of the whole earth; and from there the LORD scattered them abroad over the face of the whole earth."*

After He dispersed the nations, God chose Abram (later changed to Abraham), a man from the line of Shem, to start a new nation through which He would restore His Kingdom. With Abraham, God made an amazing covenant called the Abrahamic Covenant. It is the single most important covenant in the Bible, so it is imperative to understand it. Its importance is based upon the promises of the covenant, the repetition of it and the implementation and ultimate fulfillment.

To this point of human history, God had worked with the entire human race. From here on, the Old Testament becomes a **Jewish book**. Other nations are included only as they relate to Israel. The Abrahamic Covenant is bound up inseparable with the history of the nation Israel and the restoration of God's earthly rule. Because this covenant is so crucial, we will spend much of this chapter understanding it and its impact on the rest of God's Kingdom purpose.

1A. THE CHARACTERISTICS OF THE ABRAHAMIC COVENANT

1B. It is eternal (Gen. 13:15; 15:17-21; 17:7,13,19; 1 Chron. 16:16-17; Ps. 105:9-10)

When the Abrahamic Covenant was ratified in Genesis 15, God alone walked through the pieces of the animals. It was a blood covenant and when one entered such a covenant, animals were slain and cut in two halves and placed opposite each other. The persons entering the covenant would walk between the carcasses signifying what would happen to them should they fail to live up to their part of the covenant. In this way, God was demonstrating that if He failed to keep His covenant with Abraham, He would die. Since God is faithful to His word and is immortal (1 Tim. 1:17), this cannot happen. God also described the covenant as "everlasting," which is the same Hebrew term used to describe Him as the "Everlasting God." The covenant is eternal, meaning the people to whom it was given, and the provisions and promises are too! Your understanding of the Abrahamic Covenant, if it is to be faithful to the Scriptures, must include the eternal nature of the promises given Abraham. Put in question form, "will the promises God made Abraham have any fulfillment in the future?" "Are those promises eternal, or only to be set aside by God?" The covenant is eternal, and God is faithful to His word. Israel's behavior has nothing to do with the ultimate fulfillment of its promises.

2B. It is unconditional (Gen. 12:1-3; 13:14-17; 15:1-21; 17:1-27; 18:18-19; 22:1-18)

God alone initiated, promised and ratified the covenant. In the verses above, God uses the personal pronoun "I" twenty-four times. Never is Abraham asked to do anything – this covenant is an unconditional covenant, because it is totally dependent on God's faithfulness to Himself. To **enjoy** the covenant blessings requires faith and obedience (Gen. 15:4-6; 17:1-2). However, enjoying the covenant blessings is not the same as entering the covenant. The covenant is **made** by the grace of God and **enjoyed** by the obedience of man.

As an illustration, marriages are normally entered into unconditionally. Grooms and brides make promises to do certain things for their beloved with no strings attached. However, if they truly want to enjoy the covenant relationship, they will do certain things that please the one to whom they have covenanted their love.

3B. It is foundational to the rest of God's program.

The entire history of the world after Abraham is within the Abrahamic Covenant. All God's works with the nations are grounded in this covenant, as are all other covenants God makes with Israel and the church. Each is an expansion or application of the provisions of the Abrahamic covenant. The Land, Davidic and New Covenants are all major, yet each is only a part of the Abrahamic Covenant.

2A. THE REVELATION OF THE ABRAHAMIC COVENANT

God progressively reveals more and more of the covenant promises to Abraham as they walk together. See these key Scriptures in Genesis 12:1-3; 13:14-17; 15:1-21; 17:1-27; 18:18-19; 22:17-18.

PROGRESSIVE REVELATION OF THE ABRAHAMIC COVENANT
The covenant was **given** in Gen. 11:29-32; Josh. 24:2-4; Acts 7:2-4
The covenant was **repeated** in Gen. 12:1-3
The covenant was **reaffirmed** in Gen. 13:14-18
The covenant was **ratified** in Gen. 15:1-19
The covenant was **further clarified** in Gen 17 and 22

God also reaffirmed the covenant to <u>Isaac</u> (Gen. 26:2-4), and Jacob (Gen. 28:13-15; 35:11-12 and 46:3) and reminded Moses of it (Exod. 3:6-8; 6:28). It is referred to or repeated in almost every book of the Bible after Genesis. God's original blessing to mankind (Gen. 1:28) will be restored and fulfilled through Abram and his offspring. The seventh promise is quoted in Acts 3:25 with reference to Peter's Jewish listeners – Abram's physical descendants – and in Galatians 3:8 with reference to Paul's Gentile listeners – Abram's spiritual descendants.

3A. THE PROVISIONS OF THE COVENANT

When you chart this covenant, you find several key areas.

THE ABRAHAMIC COVENANT		
Parties: God, Abraham and his seed	**Type**: Unconditional	**Main Texts**: Gen. 12:1-3; 15:1-19
THE PROMISES WITHIN THE COVENANT TO ABRAHAM		
1. I will make you a great nation. 2. I will bless you. 3. I will make your name great.	4. You will be a blessing. 5. I will bless those who bless you.	6. Whoever curses you, I will curse. 7. All peoples on earth will be blessed through you.
THE EXTENTS OF THE PROMISES		
Personal Provisions Abraham	*National Provisions* Physical Seed	*Universal Provisions* All peoples
Limited Application	**Universal Application**	
The personal promises made to Abraham The national promises made to the seed	The blessings and curses (Gen. 12:3a, 27:29; Num. 24:9) Some of the promises made to the seed The universal blessing (Acts 3:25-26; Gal. 3:8-9, 13-14)	
Theocratic Application		
Those "in Christ" become Abraham's spiritual seed (Gal. 3:6-9). Christ, the ultimate ruling seed, will govern the earth perfectly in the Millennium (Isa. 9:6-7) Christ will make Israel a great nation when they become the "head" of the nations in the Millennium (Deut. 28:13) Christ will now allot national Israel her promised land in the Millennium (Gen. 15:8, Ezek. 47:13-48:35) Christ will fulfill the curses and blessings (Matt. 25:31-46)		

4A. THE SEED WITHIN THE COVENANT[4]

God officially ratified the covenant in Genesis 15. Depending on your translation, God refers to Abraham's "seed" or "offspring" in Genesis 15:1-5. Since the seed

---

4. Baughman, Ray E. *The Kingdom of God Visualized;* (Chicago, IL; Moody Press), Adapted from pages 24-26

figures so prominently in the covenant, we must understand this concept. In reference to descendants in the Old Testament, "seed" is always singular. When that seed is compared to the stars or the dust, it is used in a collective sense.

Scripture described five "seed" in reference to Abraham. The chart on the following page shows the "seed" in graphic form."

>1B. **Natural**, physical offspring (Gen. 25:1-4). This would include any and every descendant of Abraham, including Ishmael, the sons of Keturah (Abraham's wife after Sarah died and any children he fathered through his concubines). Think of a "family tree." This seed would involve all the branches of Abraham's family tree.
>
>2B. **National**, seed (the nation Israel) believing or unbelieving (Gen. 21:11-13; Rom. 9:6-9). This seed would include only the descendants of Abraham through Isaac and Jacob. It would exclude all others, including Ishmael, Esau and more. It would include only those who were later known as the twelve tribes of Israel. Again, think of a "family tree" – this designation only includes certain branches of the tree, not the entire tree.
>
>3B. The **Ruling** seed, or the "seed who will rule" (Gen. 17:6; 28:1215; 49:10-12; 2 Sam. 7:12-16). This designation of "seed" would exclude eleven of the twelve tribes of Israel and include only certain members of the tribe of Judah, who would qualify to rule as kings. Again, using the tree analogy, this seed would refer to a single branch of the tree.
>
>4B. The **Spiritual** seed, those who are "in Christ" (Gal. 3:6-9, 14). Paul, in the New Testament, applies this seed to all who, like Abraham, are people of faith. We are his "spiritual children" because, like our "spiritual father" we too came to faith in Jesus and are thus part of the same family. This would not only include Gentiles who come to faith but also all descendants of Abraham who were of the

natural, national and ruling seed who also believed God's promise, as did Abraham. As Romans 11:17 states, the
Gentile believers are branches that have been grafted into this tree.

5B. **Jesus Christ**, "the seed" (Gal. 3:15-16). The New Testament used this term to only apply to Jesus. He is not merely "a" seed but "the" seed. He was/is the promised seed of the woman, from Abraham and Judah, who would crush the serpent's head (Gen. 3:15) by His death and resurrection and would also reign eternally as Judah's descendant and, David's son.

Abraham's Seed

Based on Genesis 3:15 & 12:1-3

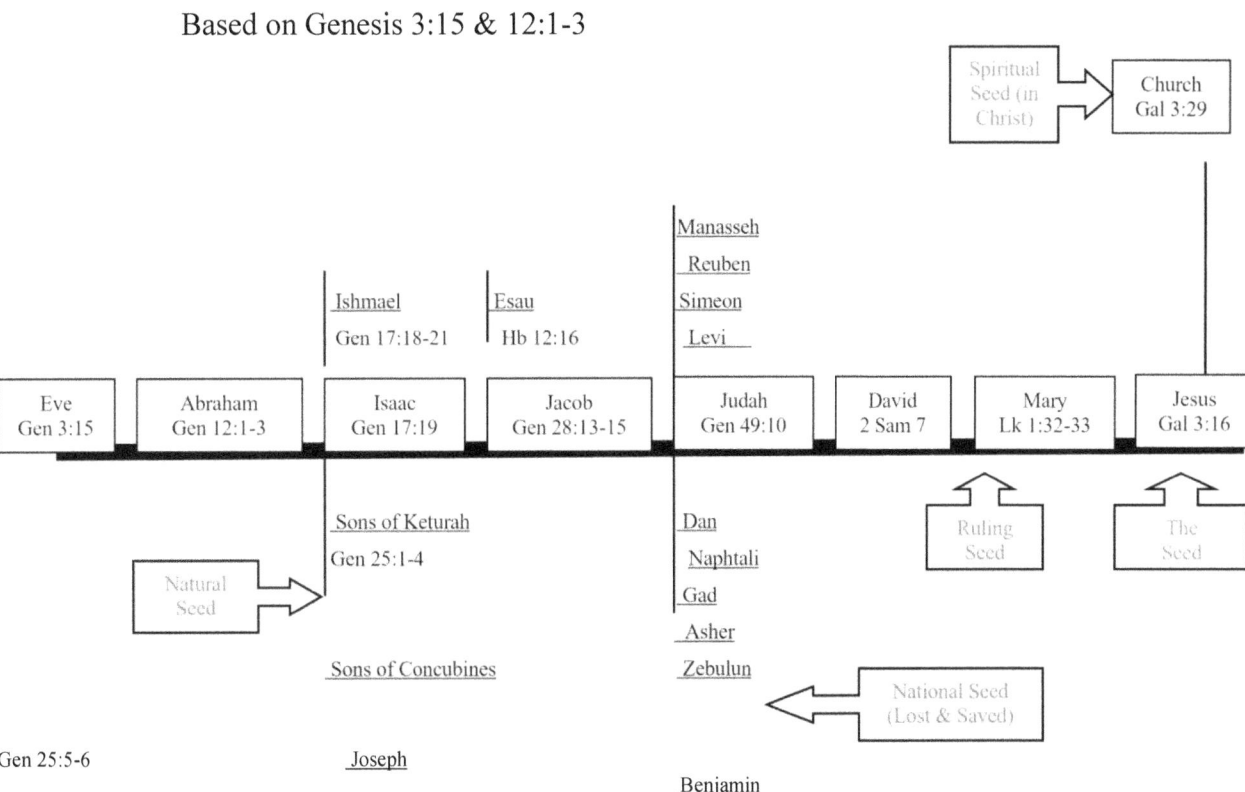

Thus, the seed God promised to come from Eve has now been more **progressively revealed**. He will also be from the line of Shem (Gen. 9:26). God then chose Abraham, a descendant to Shem to be the recipient of this covenant (Gen. 11:29-32). Tracking Abraham's "seed" through the Bible leads us ultimately to the Lord Jesus Christ.

5A. THE EARLY OUTWORKING OF THE COVENANT IN ISRAEL'S HISTORY (Gen. 15:1 – Exod. 18:27)

In the Abrahamic covenant, God had revealed four things about Abraham's descendants (Gen. 15:13-14). First, they would become **strangers** in a country not their own (13a). Second, they would be **enslaved 400 years** in that land (13b). Third, God would **punish** the enslaving nation (14a). Finally, God promised that they would come out with great **possessions** (14b). Genesis 25:12 – Exodus 18:27 details the **fulfillment** of these two verses.

After Abraham's death, God reaffirmed the Abrahamic Covenant to Isaac (Gen. 26:1-6) and Jacob (Gen. 28:10-15). Although they were a covenant family, Jacob and his sons were not **practically righteous**. Indeed, they were almost overcome by the paganism in the land of Canaan. Therefore, in sovereign grace, God acted to preserve His people through Joseph. Therefore, Joseph's story takes so many chapters in Genesis (37 – 50). God preserved the chosen family by removing them from the wicked land and sending them to Egypt where they could increase and be readied for national life.

In Egypt, God kept the first promise about Abram's seed: Israel became strangers in a country not their own (Gen. 15:13; 46:1-27). God expressed His sovereign rule using the sinfulness of Jacob's sons and their need for food to fulfill the prophecy. Genesis ends with the nation in Egypt, prospering, yet looking for God to keep the promise He made to Abraham (Gen. 50:22-26).

Some years after the death of Joseph, As God had predicted, Israel became slaves to the Egyptians (Gen 15:13; Exod. 1:8-14). Israel had lived in the spiritual kingdom of darkness in Egypt for over 400 years when God remembered His covenant (Exod. 2:24-25). God revealed Himself to Moses in Midian (Exod. 3:1-5), appointed Moses His theocratic administrator, and sent him back to Egypt to rescue his covenant people (Exod. 3:6-10).

But before God delivered Israel, He severely punished the Egyptians with the plagues for their mistreatment of His covenant people (Exod. 7-12). The 10 plagues established Moses' **authority** (Exod. 4:1-9) and demonstrated God's sovereign faithfulness (7:5, 17; 8:10 etc.). Again, He did so because He is faithful to His covenant, and in this case, He punished those who cruelly enslaved Israel for 400 years (Gen. 12:3).

God graciously redeemed Israel as a people through the Passover. Their faith was evidenced in a blood sacrifice and obedience (Exod. 12:7, 13, 23). God "passed over" to protect those of faith and "passed over" to judge those who did not believe. God remembered His promise to Abraham and delivered Israel from Egyptian bondage. Israel came out with full hands, just as God had promised, right down to the exact day He had predicted (Gen. 15:14; Exod. 12:40-41).

Israel was now a redeemed nation. Abraham's descendants were free from slavery and under the blood sacrifice (Exod. 12). God determined to be their King and to make them a great and unique nation. God protected Israel through a cloud by day and a pillar of fire by night (Exod. 14:13-28) and provided for her through manna six days per week for forty years (Exod. 15:23-26; 16:1-6 and 17:5-6)! Israel responded with worship and praise as well as disobedience and disbelief (Exod. 15-18).

This ends the **Dispensation of Promise** and sets the stage for the **Mosaic Covenant** and **dispensation of Law** that starts in Exodus 19. We can summarize the age of promise and that period of progressive revelation as follows:

DISPENSATION OF PROMISE						
Man's Responsibility	God's Covenant	Theocratic Ruler	Man's Failure	God's Judgment	God's Gracious Revelation	Main Text
Rule Earth	Adamic	Adam	Submit to Satan	Fall	Woman's Seed	Gen. 1-3
Look for Seed		Individuals	Satanic corruption	Flood	Line of Shem	Gen. 4-9
Govern Earth	Noahic	Government	Human unity	Scattering	Universal blessing	Gen. 10-12
Relate to Israel	Abrahamic	Patriarchs	Enslaved Israel	Plagues	Future of the World	Gen. 12, 15, 17, 22

CHAPTER 6 REVIEW/SUMMARY

1. The Abrahamic Covenant is eternal, unconditional and foundational to all God will do thereafter.

2. The Abrahamic Covenant was mentioned in Genesis 12, reaffirmed in Genesis 13, ratified in Genesis 15 and reaffirmed to Isaac (Genesis 26) and Jacob (Genesis 28).

3. The term "seed", when referring to Abraham's descendants is used in many ways. They include:

- His Natural seed, that is everyone who was physically related to him (Genesis 25:1-4).
- His National seed, that is only those related to him through Isaac and Jacob (Genesis 21:11-13; Romans 9:6-9).
- His Ruling seed, the "kingly" line through Judah (his great-grandson), Genesis 17:6; 28:12-15; 49:10-12; 2 Samuel 7:12-16
- His Spiritual seed, all who believe in Christ, as Abraham did, and are, therefore, "in Christ" (Galatians 3:6-9).
- THE Seed, Jesus Christ, the fulfillment of the promises of the covenant, Galatians 3:15, 16.

Chapter 7: A KINGDOM OF PRIESTS
1445-970 BC
Exodus 19 – 2 Samuel 7

God's purpose is to reestablish His theocracy over all the earth through Abraham's descendants. Those racial descendants of Abraham are known collectively as Israel or the Jews. From Exodus 19 to 2 Samuel 7 we find Israel's **national establishment**, her **sinful fragmentation** and the **beginning of her rule by kings**. This section of Scripture contains two new covenants and the start of a new dispensation.

Every nation needs a government and a ruler to prevent chaos and to, hopefully, provide an environment where moral law is the rule. Israel was different at her **national birth**. God designed her national purpose; God wrote her **constitution** and **legal system** and God served as her King. She was to be a model for the other nations to follow. This marvelous series of events is rooted in Exodus 19 where we find the Mosaic Covenant (19:134:28) and the start of the Law dispensation (John 1:17).

- Israel's **King was God Himself**. She is the only national theocracy that history has known.

  "You yourselves have seen what I did to the Egyptians, and *how* I bore you on eagles' wings, and brought you to Myself. Now then, if you will indeed obey My voice and keep My covenant, then you shall be My own possession among all the peoples, for all the earth is Mine" Exodus 19:4, 5

- She **was to be a <u>kingdom</u> of priests** and a **<u>missionary</u> people** to the nations (Exod. 19:5b-6; Josh. 4:21-24; Isa. 43:8-13). Below, Joshua 4:21-24 is quoted:

  > He said to the sons of Israel, "When your children ask their fathers in time to come, saying, 'What are these stones?' then you shall inform your children, saying, 'Israel crossed this Jordan on dry ground.' For the LORD your God dried up the waters of the Jordan before you until you had crossed, just as the LORD your God had done to the Red Sea, which He dried up before us until we had crossed; that all the peoples of the earth may know that the hand of the LORD is mighty, so that you may fear the LORD your
  > God forever."

- Her **constitution was the conditional Mosaic covenant** at Sinai (Exod. 19:5-6; 20:1).

God had redeemed Israel from Egypt. His people were obligated to their Redeemer, but because of their years in Egypt, they were ignorant of how to fulfill their obligation. The books of Exodus through Deuteronomy, known collectively as "The Law" prescribes those obligations.

1A. THE DISPENSATION OF LAW

The Mosaic Covenant is the basis for the dispensation of Law. John 1:17, states, "For the Law was given through Moses; grace and truth were realized through Jesus Christ." The Law focused God's purpose in a single nation, Israel. It is crucial to realize that you were never under the Law and that its **<u>regulatory</u>** aspects never specifically apply to you.

THE DISPENSATION OF LAW	
Israel's Responsibility	**Israel's Failure**
1. To trust God's promise to Abraham (Gal. 3:15-18). 2. To be an earthly kingdom of priests (Exod. 19:6) 3. To mediate God's rule to the whole earth (Exod. 19:1-5)	1. She trusted works of the Law rather than God's grace through faith. 2. She never became a kingdom of priests 3. She failed to meditate God's rule globally.
God's Judgment on Israel	
He scattered her among the nations. See Deut. 26:16-30:10 and Lev. 26	

2A. THE PURPOSE OF THE MOSAIC COVENANT[5]

It is important to understand that the Mosaic Covenant was made with a nation formed by blood sacrifice (Exod. 12). However, a covenant *nation* does not mean that every *individual* was/is redeemed (Rom. 9:6-9).

National formation is corporate whereas redemption is **individual**.

Not all of those who left Egypt were subject of God's spiritual kingdom. Some were satanic enemies of God's theocracy of redeemed subjects, designated the "mixed multitude" or the "rabble". This rabble was probably a group of people who lived in Egypt and joined Israel as they departed from Egypt. They later demonstrated their unbelief by rejecting Moses' authority and rebelling against God's rule (Exod. 12:38; Num. 11:4). Along with Israel's disbelief and disobedience, they proved to be quite a problem for Moses.

Because Israel was largely ignorant of God's person and purposes, they needed a special and specific revelation to direct them in how to walk with

---

5. Pentecost, adapted 82-100

Him. Remember, they had just been freed from 400 years of slavery in Egypt and had been surrounded by the many gods of Egypt. It is critical to understand that the Law of Moses was *never intended to **give life**, only to **regulate** the life of Israel.*

Galatians 3:21, 25 states, "Is the Law then contrary to the promises of God? May it never be! For if a law had been given which was able to impart life, then righteousness would indeed have been based on law. But now that faith has come, we are no longer under a tutor."

God gave the Mosaic Law for three primary purposes:

> 1B. The Law was to be **Israel's national constitution** (Exod. 19:3-8). Just as the United States has a national constitution, the Law was Israel's constitution. When faced with questions about the legality of an activity, people naturally look to legal documents. The Law was Israel's source.
>
> 2B. The Law was to **reveal God's truth** (Rom. 3:19-20; 7:711; Lev. 26; Deut. 26:16-30:10; Rom. 7:12; 1 Pet. 1:1516). This was no ordinary code. It was not manmade, as it came directly from God through His spokesman, Moses.
>
> 3B. The Law was to **regulate a redeemed nation**, and not to redeem a people (Exod. 19:1-6; Gal. 3:15-25; Heb. 11:2829). It was to regulate the broken fellowship of the **redeemed** (Lev. 1 – 7), to reveal and regulate Israel's worship (Lev. 23), to **regulate** Israel's future Kings and prophets (Deut. 17 – 18), to reveal Israel's national history, especially regarding her ownership and enjoyment

of the land (Lev. 26; Deut. 26-30) and to reveal some aspects of the King to **come** (Deut. 18; Lk. 24:13-27).

The following chart summarizes the Mosaic Covenant:

THE MOSAIC COVENANT		
Parties: God and Israel	**Type**: Conditional	**Text**: Exod. 19:1-34:27
How God Related to Israel	**What Israel Was to Do**	
To be Israel's Redeemer King (Exod. 19:1-4, 34-27) To make Israel a kingdom of priests if they obey (Exod. 19:5-6) To bless and curse for response to His Law (Lev. 26)	To obey fully as a redeemed people (Exod. 19:5) To meditate God's truth to the nations (Exod. 19:6, 1 Kgs. 8:41-43)	
Universal Application		
The revelatory parts of the Law that show God's holiness, the character of those in fellowship with God, the person and work of Christ and the sinfulness of man still apply. The regulatory parts do not.		
Theocratic Application		
Christ fulfilled the regulatory aspects of the Law (Rom. 10:4) Christ redeems from the curse of the Law (Gal. 3:10-14)		

4A. THE LAND COVENANT AND ISRAEL'S HISTORY

The second covenant we will consider is the Land Covenant. It is called this because it describes Israel's relationship to the land of Promise. (It is often called the Palestinian Covenant by evangelical scholars). The land ***belongs to Israel*** because God gave it to them in the Abrahamic Covenant (Gen. 13:7; 13:14-17). However, ***enjoying the land*** depends on Israel's obedience to the Law. The Land Covenant is an unconditional promise that expresses the conditions to ***enjoy the land forever*** (Deut. 28 –30; see Deut. 29:1). It expands the land aspect of the Abrahamic Covenant and is termed an **eternal covenant** in Ezekiel 16:60.

Enjoying the land depends on Israel's **regeneration** and **obedience**. Because she has never been entirely saved as a nation, Israel has experienced the disciplinary aspects of the covenant (Deut. 28:58-67). Through the eras of Joshua, Judges and the Kings, even until today, the provisions of the Land Covenant govern Israel's relationship to her land. Included are the dispersions by Assyria (722BC), Babylon (586BC), and Rome (70AD). God also specified the generational aspects of disobedience and its effects on the land of promise in Deut. 29:22-28. However, when

Israel turns to God from the heart, the land will be theirs forever (30:1-10). This has never happened and awaits the return of Christ (Zech. 12:1-13:6 especially 12:6-8,10).

Perhaps an illustration from life might help. My wife inherited some land from her parents many years ago. Forty acres in rural Alabama. We own the property, but we do not enjoy the property. The reason? We don't live there and have done nothing to improve it and make it habitable. So too, Israel was given land by God, but to truly enjoy it, she needed to obey God and drive out those enemies in the land that would keep her from enjoying it.

The following chart summarizes the Land Covenant:

THE LAND COVENANT		
Parties: God and Israel	**Type**: Unconditional	**Text**: Deut. 28-30
God's Role	**Israel's Role**	
To restore Israel to the land (Deut. 30:3-5) To convert the nation of Israel (30:4-8; Rom. 11:26-27) To judge Israel's enemies (30:7) To bless Israel fully (30:9)	This covenant is unconditional. The only requirement is conversion. Since this is God's work, He will do it (30:2, Hos. 2:14-23; Ezek. 11:16-21; Zech. 12:10-13:1; Rom. 11:26-27)	
Universal Application		
Obedience brings blessing, disobedience brings discipline.		
Theocratic Application		
Christ will provide Israel's conversion at His return (Zech. 12:10-13; Rom. 11:26-27) Christ will be the King who ensures Israel's future blessings (Zech. 14).		

5A. THE MOSAIC LAW AND THE ABRAHAMIC COVENANT

How does the Mosaic Law relate to the Abrahamic Covenant? The Law came after the Abrahamic Covenant but in no way changed it (Gal. 3:17). The Mosaic and Land Covenants **apply** the Abrahamic Covenant. The Mosaic and Land Covenants are built on the Abrahamic Covenant.

The Abrahamic covenant is unconditional – entirely dependent on God for its fulfillment. However, Abraham's **national** seed can only enjoy the Abrahamic Covenant conditioned on obedience. Obedience to what? God's Law, that is, the Mosaic Covenant. The Abrahamic Covenant is the **source** of the blessings while the Law provided for **enjoyment** of the blessings in the land, conditioned on obedience.

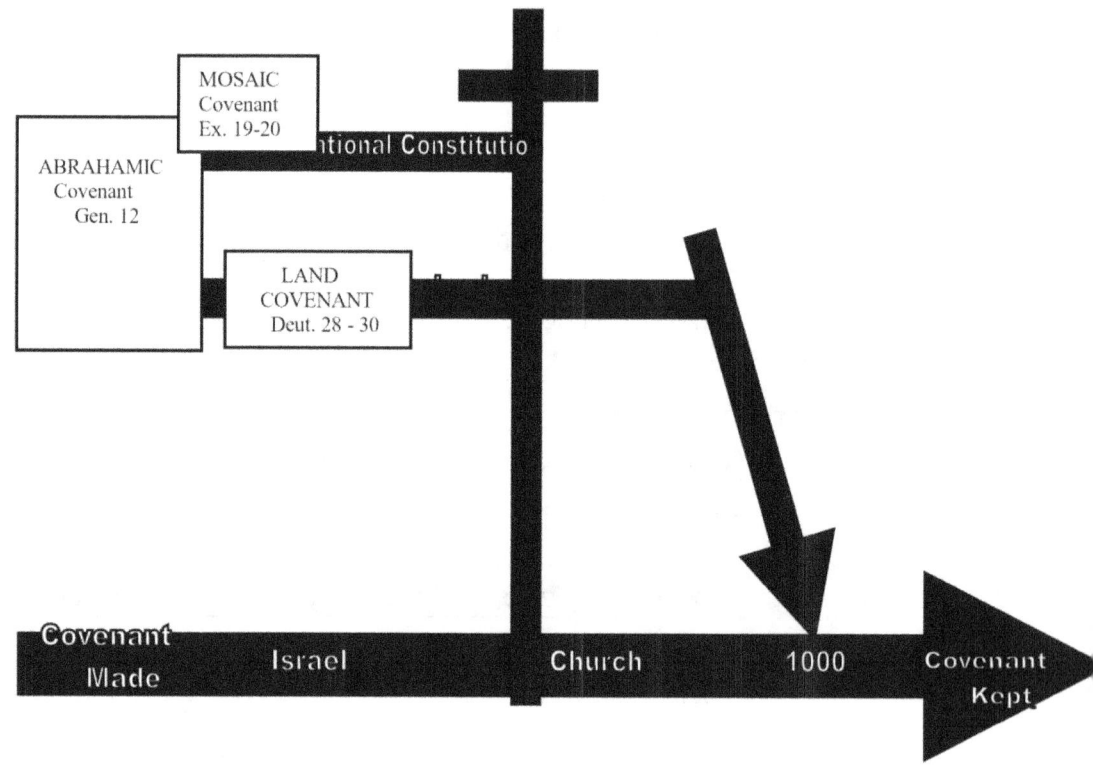

6A. THE OUTWORKING OF GOD'S KINGDOM PURPOSE

The following summarizes God's work described under various leaders during this period.

1B. Under Moses

Israel broke the Mosaic covenant almost as soon as it was made and continued to test God as she made her way toward the land (Exod. 34 – Deut. 27). Because God had promised a divine response to obedience and disobedience, this principle is demonstrated clearly in the wanderings in the book of Numbers.

2B. Under Joshua

When Moses died, God appointed Joshua as His theocratic administrator (Deut. 34:9; Josh. 1:5). God commanded Joshua to lead by appropriating the Law personally and applying it nationally (Josh. 1:6-8). Joshua assigned the land to the tribes as God instructed. God had promised Abraham and His descendants a land forever (Gen. 13:15-16; 15:18; 17:8). Since that land was her God-appointed destination, Deuteronomy anticipates Israel's possession of it. Sixty-nine times Deuteronomy mentions that Israel would "**possess**" or "**inherit**" the land. God assigned the tribes their portions of the land by sovereign grace, but He left the inheritance or enjoyment of the land up to their faithful obedience (Josh. 14:10-15).

"Inheriting the land" is a crucial phrase for understanding an important truth in both testaments. Because God gave Israel the land in the Abrahamic Covenant, it already belonged to her. However, to enjoy God's rule in the land, Israel had to trust Him, obey Him, and conquer the tribal peoples of the land. Note carefully that **entrance into the land is by grace; inheriting the land is by works**. Only a few Israelites inherited the land of promise. Most gave up too soon and never received all God promised. There is a parallel truth/principle in the New Testament: we **enter** the spiritual kingdom **by grace through faith** (John 3:1-6). We **inherit** the Millennial Kingdom **as a reward for faithful works** (Col. 3:22-4:1). The New Testament phrase, "inherit the kingdom" is to share Jesus' authority and co-reign with Him in the Millennium. Church age saints can lose their inheritance by failing to train now to reign then (Gal. 5:19-21; Eph. 5:3-7; 1 Cor. 6:9-11).

At the end of his ministry and life, Joshua called Israel to faithfulness and even summoned that generation into a covenant of commitment to God's kingship (Josh. 24:1-27).

3B. Under the Judges

After Joshua's death, the elders who had served with him administered God's rule faithfully (Judges 2:7). However, the next generation did not "know the Lord" (Judges 2:11, 15, 2023). God appointed the judges as theocratic rulers for several hundred years. God was Israel's King and He indirectly ruled through the judges (1 Sam. 12:12; Judges 8:23). It is repeated that the judges operated by the "Spirit of the Lord" rather than human strength (3:10, 6:34, 11:29, 13:25, 14:6, 19, 15:14).

The entire book of Judges is a record of God's faithfulness to keep the Land covenant as revealed in Deuteronomy 28-30. When the people groaned in repentance, God raised up a judge. When they rebelled, God chastened them, using their enemies to correct, train and discipline Israel. Judges 2:10-23 gives a good summary of this 300+ year period of Israel's history:

> All that generation also were gathered to their fathers; and there arose another generation after them who did not know the LORD, nor yet the work which He had done for Israel.
>
> Then the sons of Israel did evil in the sight of the LORD and served the Baals, and they forsook the LORD, the God of their fathers, who had brought them out of the land of Egypt, and followed other gods from *among* the gods of the peoples who were around them, and bowed themselves down to them; thus they provoked the LORD to anger. So they forsook the LORD and served Baal and the Ashtaroth. The anger of the LORD burned against Israel, and He gave them into the hands of plunderers who plundered them; and He sold them into the
>
> hands of their enemies around *them*, so that they co

sold no longer stand before their enemies. Wherever they went, the hand of the LORD was against them for evil, as the LORD had spoken and as the LORD had sworn to them, so that they were severely distressed. Then the LORD raised up judges who delivered them from the hands of those who plundered them. Yet they did not listen to their judges, for they played the harlot after other gods and bowed themselves down to them. They turned aside quickly from the way in which their fathers had walked in obeying the commandments of the LORD; they did not do as *their fathers*. When the LORD raised up judges for them, the LORD was with the judge and delivered them from the hand of their enemies all the days of the judge; for the LORD was moved to pity by their groaning because of those who oppressed and afflicted them. But it came about when the judge died, that they would turn back and act more corruptly than their fathers, in following other gods to serve them and bow down to them; they did not abandon their practices or their stubborn ways. So the anger of the LORD burned against Israel, and He said, "Because this nation has transgressed My covenant which I commanded their fathers and has not listened to My voice, I also will no longer drive out before them any of the nations which Joshua left when he died, in order to test Israel by them, whether they will keep the way of the LORD to walk in it as their fathers did, or not." So, the LORD allowed those nations to remain, not driving them out quickly; and He did not give them into the hand of Joshua. *Judges 2:10-23*

Ruth occurs near the end of this era. It shows how God ruled and overruled to prepare for the arrival of His king, David (Ruth 4:13-22). Despite the strong presence of Satan's false kingdom (Judges 21:25), God expressed His restoring purpose to rule through the Judges. The last judge he raised up was Samuel.

4B. Under Samuel

Samuel was both the **last judge** and the **first prophet** since Moses. He fulfilled a critical role in Israel's history (1 Sam.

3:19-20). He was the one through whom a transition from **theocracy** to **monarchy** occurred. Under Samuel, God's rule began to be expressed through a human king. Samuel anointed both Saul and David as Israel's first two kings.

First Samuel 8:1 informs us that Samuel appointed his sons as judges. However, this was wrong for two reasons. First, God did not appoint them, Samuel did. Second, they were not Spirit led men but part of the kingdom of darkness (1 Sam. 8:3).

Because the elders knew this, they requested a king (1 Sam. 8:5).

Appealing for a king was not sinful in itself – the Pentateuch declared that Israel would have a King (Gen. 17:6; 49:10; Deut. 17:14-20). However, their motivation for the request was wrong for two reasons. First, it was not God's intent that Israel **be like the other nations** (Exod. 19:3; 1 Sam. 8:5). Second, the method for deliverance from Israel's enemies was **repentance** rather than unified leadership and military presence (Deut. 30:2-4; 1 Sam. 8:19-20; 9:16). Thus, wanting a king was not sinful. But, rejecting God's method for deliverance and purpose for Israel was rejecting His Kingship (1 Sam. 8:7-8; 12:12-25). When the first king was anointed, he was from the tribe of Benjamin rather than Judah (1 Sam. 9:1; 10:1), indicating that he was not the **promised** king (Gen. 49:10).

Saul's primary role as the anointed theocratic ruler was to obey God. Because of his pride, Saul thought he was above the Law and could disobey with impunity. God judged Saul because he repeatedly disobeyed Him (1 Sam. 13:7-15). Consequently,

God rejected him as king (1 Sam. 15:22-23) and had Samuel anoint David as king (1 Sam. 16:12-13).

> In preparation for the next section, read Chapter 8 of this book, along with 2 Samuel 7 and Jeremiah 31.

CHAPTER 7 REVIEW/SUMMARY

1. Israel was different than all the other nations in history. She was chosen by God to be the nation through whom He would bring the Messiah and give most of His special revelation. It was to Israel that God wrote and gave her a constitution and legal system.

2. Israel's king was God; thus, she was the only theocracy in human history.

3. Israel was to be a kingdom of priests and to be a missionary people to the other nations she had contact with.

4. God gave the law to Israel to regulate the lives of a REDEEMED people, NOT to redeem a people.

5. The land God promised Israel was unconditionally given, but enjoyment of the land was dependent upon obedience to God (Deut. 28-30).

6. Inheritance/possession of the land was a matter of obedience.

7. Israel wanted a king in order to be like all the surrounding nations she interacted with and for the king to deliver Israel from her enemies through military might. God's prescribed method of victory for Israel was through repentance of sin.

Chapter 8: FROM JERUSALEM TO BABYLON AND BACK

970-400 BC

2 Samuel 7 – Malachi

When Israel requested a king, they attempted to do God's work in man's way and reaped sad consequences. Their first king was Saul, whose reign was marked by frequent disobedience. This resulted in **disinheritance** and loss of blessing and God replaced Saul with David. Saul founded the monarchy, David united it, Solomon expanded it and the remaining kings **ruined** it. At the heart of the monarchy is the Davidic Covenant.

1A. THE DAVIDIC COVENANT

David's **victory over Goliath** marked him out as God's enabled theocratic ruler. In response to God's further blessings over the next years, David wanted to build God an earthly house in which God would dwell. David realized that God was faithful to His promises, therefore he wished to honor the Lord by building Him a temple (2 Sam. 7:1-2). Instead, God made a gracious covenant with David to build his house (It is important to note that in this passage, the term "house" is employed in two ways. David wanted to build a "house"/structure/temple for God, but God said He would build a "house" – line of kings – for David with the last one reigning forever)! God had promised Abraham a land, seed and blessing. The land aspect was specified in the Land Covenant. In the Davidic Covenant God applies the seed promises of the Abrahamic Covenant. This covenant contains several provisions recorded in 2 Samuel 7:8-16. Because the Davidic Covenant is so important, it is mentioned or alluded to on many other occasions (cf. Isaiah

9:6, 7; Jeremiah 23:5, 6; Daniel 7:13, 14; Hosea 3:4, 5; Amos 9:11; and Zech. 14:4-9).

THE DAVIDIC COVENANT		
Parties: God, David, Solomon & Israel	**Type**: Unconditional	**Text**: 2 Sam. 7:8-16
God's Role		**Israel's Role**

To keep covenant with **David**: A
    great name (9)
    Rest from all enemies (11a)
    An eternal house or dynasty (11b, 16)
    A son to succeed him (12-15)
    An eternal kingdom (16)
    An eternal throne (16)
To keep covenant with **Solomon**:
    Establish his kingdom (12)
    He would build the Temple (13)
    Establish his throne forever (13)
    Chastised for disobedience (14-15)
To keep covenant with **Israel**: A permanent place (10a)
    Rest from enemies (10b)
		This covenant is unconditional. It's important to grasp that the covenant does not say the throne will always be **occupied**, only that David's descendants will endure forever. The throne may or may not be occupied at given time due to obedience or disobedience (cf. Deut. 28-30). Chastisement may cause the throne itself to be unoccupied, but there shall never lack one whose right it is to sit on that throne (2 Sam. 7:14-15; Ps. 89:30-36; Jer. 33:17). Since this is God's promise, He will do it ("I will" seven times in the covenant).

Theocratic Application		
Christ will be the ultimate Son of David who reigns forever over David's house, throne and kingdom (Lk. 1:30-33). Christ will resurrect David who will be Israel's Prince / Shepherd in the Millennium (Ezek. 34:23-26; 37:24-27)		

Through David, a kingdom of peace and righteousness will be established over Israel in the land that God previously promised them. This covenant will be literally fulfilled in the future Millennium when David is resurrected as Israel's prince and Israel is redeemed and receives her land (Ezek. 34:24; 37:24). Christ, David's ultimate Son, will reign on David's throne. The Davidic Covenant is referred to or repeated throughout the Old Testament prophetic books. This demonstrates that Israel anticipated God keeping that promise, and it teaches us that the promise still awaits fulfillment.

The Davidic Covenant will have a literal and complete fulfillment. Some portions have already been fulfilled (e.g., David's son, Solomon, ruled and was chastised by God). David himself believed it would have a literal fulfillment (2 Sam. 23:5). Additionally, its literal fulfillment was emphasized by the prophets (1 Kings 1:30-37). Finally, the New Testament emphasizes a literal fulfillment with approximately fifty-nine references to the Davidic Covenant.

2A. THE DECLINE OF THE MONARCHY

Solomon, David's son and successor, sowed the seeds of national destruction in his reign. His response to God's grace and revelation with a long, slow descent into disobedience terribly weakened the kingdom.

Following Solomon's death, his son Rehoboam unwisely and arrogantly split the kingdom (1 Kgs. 12). Jeroboam, who had been Solomon's commander of the army, led a rebellion and caused a split in the nation and ruled the northern 10 tribes, called Israel. Rehoboam remained king over the southern tribes of Judah and Benjamin, known as Judah. Jeroboam's kingdom was a satanic false rule (1 Kgs. 12:25-13:4). In faithfulness to the Land Covenant (Deut. 28), God began to judge. Throughout the history of both kingdoms, God used the prophets to summon them to repentance and promise them blessings. Twenty kings ruled Israel from the time of the divided kingdom until they went into captivity to Assyria in 722-721 BC. All twenty of them were characterized as evil, though some more so than others. The southern kingdom had twenty-five kings after the division of the kingdom. They had only a handful of godly kings who initiated reforms/revivals. Due to increasing ungodliness, Judah was defeated by Babylon and deported three times in 606-605, 597 and 586 BC. Thus, God faithfully applied the final discipline prophesied in Deuteronomy 28 and preached by his prophets.

3A. THE ROLE OF THE PROPHETS

The prophets had two primary tasks in the theocracy. One was to call Israel back to covenant faithfulness. That is they were **forthtellers**, preachers who reminded Israel of God's greatness and challenged her to fulfill the Mosaic Covenant. Their message was to repent so that God's blessing would follow (Deut. 30:1-10). The prophet's second role was that of **foretelling**. In this role, they predicted the discipline that God would send as well as the future kingdom that would come with God's King.

In pursuing their ministry, the prophets focused on two basic audiences. Some prophets addressed themselves to the kings and people of **Israel or Judah**. Others spoke to the **foreign nations** who aligned themselves against Israel. Although God might use the Gentiles to chasten his people, they would pay a great price because God is faithful to the Abrahamic covenant.

Finally, the prophets spoke during three periods of time. Some served before Israel or Judah went into exile. Others spoke and wrote while Judah was in captivity. The third prophetic period was after the exile when some of the people returned to the land of promise. The chart below depicts these prophets within their periods.

11 **PRE-EXILIC PROPHETS** 848 – 586 BC	2 **EXILIC PROPHETS** 586 – 571 BC	3 **POST-EXILIC PROPHETS** 520-420 BC
Obadiah, Joel, Jonah, Amos, Hosea, Isaiah, Micah, Nahum, Zephaniah, Jeremiah, Habakkuk	Daniel Ezekiel	Haggai Zechariah Malachi

The prophets are often grouped into two categories, the **Minor** and **Major** prophets. These names describe the length of their books, not their importance nor the significance of their message. SEE CHART BELOW.

List of the Prophets

Major Prophets	Minor Prophets
Isaiah	Hosea
Jeremiah	Joel
(Lamentations)	Amos
Ezekiel	Obadiah
Daniel	Jonah
	Micah
	Nahum
	Habakkuk
	Zephaniah
	Haggai
	Zechariah
	Malachi

With so many prophets, we will only summarize four main themes: 1) the Servant of the Lord, 2) the New Covenant, 3) the Times of the Gentiles and 4) the Return from Exile.

4A. ISAIAH AND THE SERVANT OF THE LORD

Throughout Isaiah's prophecy, both the nation of Israel (Isa. 41:8-9) and the coming Messiah are called God's "servant" or "The Servant of the Lord."

God had selected and commissioned Israel to serve as his witness to the world (Isa. 42:18-19; 43:8-13). This mandate to be His witnesses was repeated as

Israel crossed the Jordan into Canaan (Josh. 4:21-24). Solomon sensed the importance of that commission when he prayed for all the foreigners who would visit the Temple (1 Kgs. 8:41-43). But for the most part, Israel failed in her mission, becoming just like her pagan neighbors (2 Kgs. 17:5-23; 2 Chron. 36:15-21). Isaiah presents Israel as a deaf, blind and disobedient servant who failed to fulfill her divine mission (Isa. 43:8-13).

Christians, like Israel, are to be witnesses of God's salvation (Isa. 43:10 and Acts 1:8).

Because Israel failed in her national responsibility to be God's witness to the nations, He commissioned a new Servant, an individual (Isa. 42:1-17). God announced the advent of His Chosen Servant, whom He would send to establish justice on earth (Isa. 42:1-4). God spoke directly to the Servant, commissioning Him for His task (Isa. 42:5-9). This Servant, Messiah, would bring justice and light to the Gentiles (Isa. 42:1,6; 9:2; Lk. 2:32).

Isaiah wrote four "servant songs" about the Messiah. They tell us the Servant of the Lord would:

- Bring **justice** and **light** to the Gentiles (Isa. 42:1-9)
- Restore Israel and bring **salvation** to all people (Isa. 49:1-7)
- Be obedient in **suffering** (Isa. 50:4-9)
- Be **rejected** and **killed** by Israel but **exalted** by God (Isa. 52:13 – 53:12)

We, of course, know the Servant of the Lord as Jesus Christ.

5A. JEREMIAH AND THE NEW COVENANT

The Abrahamic Covenant promises a land, a seed, and a blessing. The Land covenant explained the land aspect while the seed promise is explained in the Davidic Covenant. The Land Covenant calls for national repentance **prior to** Israel's reception of her land (Deut. 30:2,3,6,8). It promises that God will "circumcise their hearts" (Deut. 30:6). This is a figure of speech for national faith. Prior to Babylon's deportation of Judah, God promised to one day restore both her spiritual and national life (Jer. 32:37-42; Ezek. 36:24-32; 37:26). This promise of **a new spiritual life that precedes a new national life** is called the <u>**New Covenant**</u>. It develops the **blessing** aspects of the Abrahamic Covenant. Many passages, particularly in Jeremiah and Ezekiel, describe the provisions of the New Covenant. The primary passage it is in Jeremiah 31:31-34:

> "Behold, days are coming," declares the LORD, "when I will make a new covenant with the house of Israel and with the house of Judah,[32] not like the covenant which I made with their fathers in the day I took them by the hand to bring them out of the land of Egypt, My covenant which they broke, although I was a husband to them," declares the LORD. [33] "But this is the covenant which I will make with the house of Israel after those days," declares the LORD, "I will put My law within them and on their heart I will write it; and I will be their God, and they shall be My people. [34] They will not teach again, each man his neighbor and each man his brother, saying, 'Know the LORD,' for they will all know Me, from the least of them to the greatest of them," declares the LORD, "for I will forgive their iniquity, and their sin I will remember no more."

This covenant was inaugurated at Calvary and will be fully implemented at Christ's return (1 Cor. 11:23-26). There is one New Covenant with a two-fold application: First, a literal, total future fulfillment to Israel in the Millennium. Second, the church presently enjoys the spiritual provisions. The New Covenant is an eternal covenant (Isa. 61:8 and Ezek. 37:16). Though Israel has often been disobedient to it, that does not remove Israel from her covenanted position (Jer. 31:34).

SEE THE FOLLOWING CHART:

THE NEW COVENANT		
Parties: God, Israel and Judah	**Type**: Unconditional	**Text**: Jer. 31:31-34, others
God's Role		**Israel's Role**
Spiritual promises: 　New birth or regeneration (33a) 　New relationship with God (33) 　The indwelling Holy Spirit (34, (Ezek. 36:27) 　Forgiveness of sins (34b) Material promises: 　Restoration to the land (32:37, 33:11) 　Rebuilt Jerusalem (31:38-40) 　A new temple (Ezek. 37:27-28)		This covenant is eternal and unconditional, and there are no conditions for enjoying its blessings.
Universal / Theocratic Application		
Christ's death ratified the covenant, but Israel has yet to experience it (Lk. 22:19-20). He provides the spiritual blessings to all believers now (1 Cor. 11:23-2; 2 Cor 3:1-4:1). Christ will convert Israel in a day at His return (Zech. 12:10-13:6; Rom. 11:26).		

If Israel is to be converted and then dwell in her land in a righteous state, when will this happen? How will this happen? What about the nations who have conquered and captured Israel? The exilic and postexilic prophets provide answers to some of these questions.

6A. DANIEL AND THE TIMES OF THE GENTILES

Daniel and Ezekiel are the two prophets of the captivity. God gave them a prophetic overview of Israel's history from her **deportation** to her **restoration** under Messiah. Ezekiel chapters 8 and 10 describe the sins that led to Israel's destruction and deportation. Later, it outlines Israel's future restoration and the reestablishment of the kingdom. Ezekiel chapters 36 – 39 foretell Israel's regathering and spiritual rebirth. Chapters 40 –48 describe the coming kingdom when Israel is back in her land with a rebuilt temple and resurrected David the prince ruling. This will be in the Millennium.

Until then, Gentiles will dominate Israel. Jesus calls this period the "times of the Gentiles" (Lk. 21:24). The times of the Gentiles is <u>that extended period of God's discipline of Israel at the hands of Gentile</u>

nations. Since God no longer rules Israel through her kings, He now rules her through the Gentile nations. They, not a son of David, would be the **temporary** way that God administers His rule. Stated another way, the times of the Gentiles is that period when no descendant of David is sitting on a throne reigning over Israel. Daniel reveals four empires that would dominate Israel. Those four empires are the Babylonian, Persian, Greek and Roman Empires. The Roman Empire exists today in a fragmentary form and will control Jerusalem until the Messiah returns and ultimately delivers Israel (Dan. 7).

Daniel helps us grasp these "times of the Gentiles" by his prophecy of the seventy weeks in Daniel 9:20-27. Gabriel told Daniel that *"seventy weeks [sevens] are decreed for your people and your holy city"* (9:24). In Hebrew, there is no separate word for week; the word "weeks" is also translated "sevens."

As is usual when studying Scripture, context controls meaning. In Daniel, as is often the case in Jewish scriptures, the people operated on a seven-year cycle. They planted for six years and let the land rest (go fallow) the seventh year. People could become indentured servants but in the seventh year they were set free. Jacob agreed to serve his future father-in-law, Laban, for "a week" as his payment of dowry (Genesis 29:20-35). So too, here in Daniel the "sevens" are seven-year cycles.

Six things are decreed to occur during the seventy weeks: (1) to finish the transgression, (2) to make an end of sins, (3) to make reconciliation (atonement) for iniquity, (4) to bring in everlasting righteousness, (5) to seal up the vision and prophecy, and (6) to anoint the Most Holy.

The seventy weeks (or sevens) are divided into three parts. (1) From the issue of the command to restore and rebuild Jerusalem there will be seven sevens, or 49 years. (2) After sixty-two more weeks, or 434 years, the Messiah shall be cut off (Dan. 9:25-26). Daniel then prophesied (3) about a coming prince, the Antichrist, who will destroy the city and the temple in the great tribulation. He will make a covenant with Israel for one week, or seven years. In the middle of that week, he will cause their sacrifice to cease and set himself up as God to be worshipped (Dan. 9:26-27; 11:31; 2 Thess. 2:3,4; Matt. 24:15). See chart below.

TIMES OF THE GENTILES Daniel 9:24-27			
Event	Rebuild Jerusalem	Messiah Comes / Cut off	Covenant
Years	49	434	7
Prophetic Weeks	7	62	1
Passage	9:24-25a	9:25b-26a	9:26b, 27

Jesus' triumphal entry fulfilled Daniel's second prophecy to the exact day! Then, the seventy sevens were interrupted at the close of the sixtyninth week by the **crucifixion**. The unspecified interval between the sixty-ninth and the seventieth week has lasted almost 2000 years. We are living in that time now. Daniel's seventieth week will start when the Jews sign a covenant with Antichrist. Mentioned in Isaiah 28:15-18, this covenant is a "covenant with death and an agreement with hell." Daniel's 70th week is the subject of much of the Lord's Olivet Discourse in Matthew 24-25 and Revelation 5-19.

7A. THE RETURN FROM EXILE

Haggai, Zechariah and Malachi, as postexilic prophets, prophesied after the return from captivity. Malachi's one primary contribution to the progressive revelation of God's kingdom program is that Elijah will precede and announce the Messiah's arrival (Mal. 4:5). Haggai mentions the Messiah's final victory over the Gentiles in Haggai 2:2123. Zechariah, however, makes at least fourteen references to the coming Messiah and/or His Kingdom. Thus, the Old Testament closes as it opened, looking for the King and His kingdom. We can summarize the **progressive Old Testament kingdom revelation** as follows:

1B. It is based upon God's **unconditional** covenants (Gen. 1:26-28; 12:1-3; Deut. 28-30; 2 Sam. 7:8-16; Jer. 31:3140).

2B. Christ will be **King**, He is a descendant of David's family, was born of a virgin in the city of Bethlehem (Isa. 9:6; Matt. 1:23; 2 Sam. 7:16; Isa. 7:14).

3B. He will rule over **regathered** and **converted** Israel in David's restored kingdom (Deut. 30:3-6; Isa. 11:11-12; Jer. 33:7-9).

4B. Jerusalem will be His **capitol** and Israel will be **exalted** over the other nations of the earth (Ps. 72:11; Isa. 2:1-3; 55:5; Dan. 7:13-14; Zech. 8:22; cf. Rev 19:16).

5B. Righteousness, holiness, and peace will characterize his **kingdom** (Isa. 35:10; Jer. 31:28-34; Ezek. 36:24-34).

6B. Christ will **lessen** the curse. People will live longer, disease will be abolished, and there will be great agricultural productivity (Isa. 11:6-9; 32:14-16; 35:5-6; 65:20,22; Ezek. 36:34-38). The curse will not be completely abolished until after the millennium (Rev. 22:15).

7B. Satan will be **imprisoned**, and his angelic rebellion defeated and punished (Isa. 14 and Ezek. 28; cf. Rev 20:2).

8B. The Old Testament saints will be **resurrected** and will have a part in the kingdom (Dan. 12:2-3; Lk. 13:28).

The kingdom concept is traced from the first chapter of Genesis through to the concluding words of the prophets. God progressively reveals the truths that govern His kingdom and predict its future glory. That Old Testament revelation is centered in His unconditional covenants with Israel. Together, they provide the divine outline of what God will do to completely restore His earthly Kingdom and vindicate his glory. The Abrahamic Covenant is at the heart of this revelation and is the foundation for the other unconditional covenants.

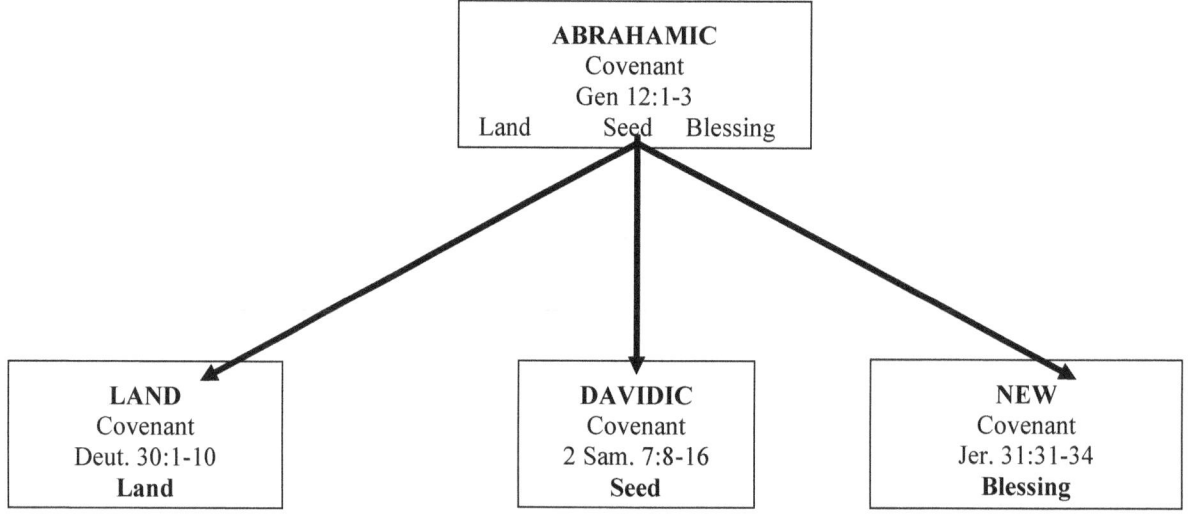

God delegates his rule through various agents. He will one day fill the earth with His glory when His Kingdom is finally reestablished (Num. 14:21; Ps. 72:19; Isa. 6:3; 11:9; Habakkuk 2:14). God's rule in the Old Testament is summarized below.

THE KINGDOM

The unifying Theme of the Old Testament		
Ruler	**Realm**	**Responsibility**
Adam	Creation	Man was to obey God and subdue nature.
Noah	Humanity	Administer justice and guard the sanctity of life through government.
Abraham	His family	1. To father a nation through whom God will rule the world 2. God promised him (a) Land, (b) Posterity, (c) Blessing
Moses and the Judges	Israel	1. God was King; Israel the subjects; the Law the constitution 2. Israel was to mediate God's truth to the nations 3. God appointed judges to rule Israel as needed
David and the Kings	Israel	1. Kings were mediators of God's rule over Israel 2. God promised David (a) dynasty, (b) throne, (c) Kingdom, (d) Eternal Rule
Prophets	Israel	1. Called the Kings and people back to the Mosaic Covenant 2. Announced God's judgment on Israel and Israel's enemies 3. Prophesied about the final form of the Kingdom
Gentiles	Israel	After the monarchial kingdom was destroyed, God placed Israel under His discipline via four Gentile empires, the Babylonian, Medo-Persian, Greek and Roman. This is the "times of the Gentiles" and will continue until Christ returns.

This closes the Old Testament and brings us to the New Testament and its progressive revelation of God's word and works.

To prepare for the next study, read Chapter 9 in this resource along with Matthew chapters 12-13 and 24-25. Write down any questions you have and be ready for discussion.

CHAPTER 8 REVIEW/SUMMARY

1. God promised to build a house/dynasty for David by means of the Davidic Covenant. David would have an heir to the throne who would rule eternally (2 Samuel 7:16).

2. Israel had a civil war and split into two nations. The northern ten tribes were often called Israel. The southern two tribes were usually referred to as Judah. Most kings from both kingdoms were wicked.

3. In faithfulness to the Land/Palestinian Covenant, God sent other nations to oppress/discipline Israel (by the Assyrians) and Judah (by the Babylonians).

4. The roles of the prophets were two-fold: To <u>Forthtell</u> – *preach* God's message; and to <u>Foretell</u> – *prophesy* the future as revealed by God.

5. The <u>three periods</u> of the major and minor prophets were pre-exilic, exilic and post-exilic.

6. The <u>four main themes</u> that emerge from the prophets are:
- Isaiah and the Servant of the Lord.
- Jeremiah and the New Covenant.
- Daniel and the Times of the Gentiles
- prophets and the Return from exile.

Chapter 9:
THE GOSPELS
6BC-30 AD

Chronologically speaking there is a 400-year gap between Malachi and Matthew. This period is often referred to as the intertestamental period. It is also often referred to as the "400 silent years". For four long centuries God did not give additional special revelation. Though there is a long gap between Malachi and Matthew, theologically and thematically, however, there is no gap or change. The New Testament picks up where the Old Testament closed. The Gospels show that God's kingdom program continues with the nation Israel and the person of Jesus. The Mosaic Covenant still governs the life of Israel in the Gospels.

1A. THE GOSPELS AND PROGRESSIVE REVELATION

The gospels are not biographies of Jesus. Rather they are <u>thematic explanations</u> of His words and works. Three gospels are very similar and are called the **synoptics** meaning "**same viewpoint**." These gospels are Matthew, Mark and Luke, each of which is addressed to believers. John, the fourth gospel, takes a different perspective on the life of Christ and writes to win people to Christ. The following chart summarizes the Gospel emphases.

THE GOSPEL ACCOUNTS

	MATTHEW	MARK	LUKE	JOHN
Character of Christ	King	Servant	Son of Man	Son of God
OT Connection	Son of David 2 Sam. 7	Servant of the Lord Isa. 42 – 53	Son of Adam Gen. 3, Dan. 7:13	The Lord Himself Isa. 6
Kingdom Point	To Rule the Kingdom **as promised**	To Bring the Kingdom **by submission**	Fulfill Man's Purpose – **Rule Earth**	Vindicate God's **nature – glory**
Covenants referred to	Mosaic, Abrahamic, Davidic, New	Mosaic, Abrahamic, Davidic, New	Mosaic, Abrahamic, Davidic, New	Mosaic, Abrahamic, Davidic, New
Primary Audience	Jewish Believers	Roman Believers	Greek Believers	Unbelievers

If Christ is to bring God's kingdom, He must be a unique person. That is exactly what the gospels demonstrate. He is the promised King who offers the promised Kingdom to Israel. Although rejected, He continues God's Kingdom work. He develops an interim form of His Kingdom and ratifies the New Covenant by his death and resurrection. Until His return, the church is to extend His <u>spiritual kingdom</u> globally by discipling the nations. As this good news unfolds, it does so around Jesus' birth, life, ministry, death, and victorious resurrection.

2A. THE GOSPELS AND THE PERSON OF THE KING

1B. The gospel of John makes it clear that Jesus is God who became man (John 1:1-14). The gospel of Mark begins with a statement that Jesus is the Son of God, while Matthew and Luke develop the historical context around His miraculous birth. The genealogies reveal insights about Christ's birth as it initiates or provides for fulfillment of various aspects of Israel's covenants.

THE GENEALOGIES AND THE UNCONDITIONAL COVENANTS				
	ABRAHAMIC	LAND	DAVIDIC	NEW

| Matthew | 1:1, 17 | | 1:1, 17, 2:1-8 | 1:21 |
| Luke | 1:14-17,26-38; 2:21 | 1:14-17, 31-33 | 1:26-38,46-55,67-76; 2:11 | 1:77-78; 2:10-11; 2:22-35 |

2B. The preparation for the king

1C. John the Baptist

Before introducing us to Jesus himself, the synoptics tell us about his forerunner, John the Baptist. All three quote Isaiah 40:3-5 to identify John with God's prophesied program. John, Messiah's forerunner, came with similar clothing, spirit, and power that Elijah exhibited (Malachi 3:1, 4:5; Matt. 3:1-12; 11:13-14; 17:12-13; Mk. 1:1-8; 9:11-13; Lk. 1:17).

The Jewish people, led by the Pharisees, believed that God's choice of them, their circumcision, outward conformity to the traditions, and the Old Testament promises guaranteed their acceptance by God and entrance into His kingdom (see John 8:33-39). Tragically, they misdiagnosed their most significant problem! They believed their most pressing problem was the Roman government and its intrusive policies and abusive taxation. The Kingdom they looked for was strictly a coming earthly, political, and military rule. They thought they needed no spiritual renewal; they only needed the King to come and destroy Rome. Therefore, both John and Jesus began their message with "Repent!" John's message was two-fold (1) "**repent**, for the kingdom of heaven is at hand" (Matt. 3:1) and (2) "**Behold** the Lamb of God who takes away the sin of the world" (John 1:29). John, like all of God's prophets, had both a national and an individual message. He announced God's promised kingdom and Israel's need to prepare for it (Isa. 40; 60-66). To be a nation of priests, restored to her land free of Gentile **domination**, Israel needed spiritual cleansing (Exod. 19:6; Lev. 16:4; Deut. 30:1-10).

This message explains John's baptism. It was a sign that one was **prepared** for the kingdom as described in the Land Covenant. John's baptism was much different from believer's baptism. Our baptism looks back to Christ's work and ahead to our new life. John's baptism looked ahead to Christ's cleansing, judgment, and Kingdom.

JOHN'S BAPTISM
It was **based on** repentance and confession (Mk. 1:4-5)
It was **prompted by** national and individual uncleanness (Lk. 3:7-14)
It was **designed to** prevent judgment (Lk. 3:7-9; Matt. 3:7-12)
It **anticipated** forgiveness through the Messiah and the New Covenant (Matt. 3:11; Mk. 1:8; Lk. 3:15-18; John 1:26-31)

As John worked to prepare the nation for Messiah's coming, the fulfillment of the Land Covenant and the inauguration of the New Covenant, Jesus also came to him to be baptized. Why was Jesus baptized? He did not need or submit to baptism for the reasons why believers are baptized. Since this is so, why did He submit to the procedure?

2C. **Jesus' Baptism**

When Jesus came to be baptized, John knew that Jesus did not need neither preparation for the Kingdom nor any forgiveness. John even confessed that he needed the "baptism in Spirit" that only Jesus could give (Mt 3:13-14). Jesus' baptism accomplished five things:

JESUS' BAPTISM
Released John to **publicly recognize and announce** Jesus as Messiah (John 1:3334).
Identified Jesus with the **believing minority** who sought God's kingdom (Lk. 3:21a).
Anointed Jesus with the Holy Spirit to **enable** Him as Messiah (Lk. 3:22; Acts 10:38).
Confirmed that Jesus is God's Son the **Savior-King** (Lk. 3:22b; Ps. 2:7; Isa. 42:1).
Fulfilled all righteousness by **consecrating** Jesus to his ministry (Matt. 3:15; Lev. 16:4).

3C. Jesus' Temptation

Following his baptism, the Spirit led Jesus into the wilderness to be tested by Satan (Matt. 4:1-11). This renewed the conflict between the prince of the kingdom of darkness and God's appointed King. Note that Satan recognized Christ's **right** to a worldwide Kingdom and offered it to him (Matt. 4:8-9; Lk. 4:6). Satan attacked Jesus' **method** of receiving the kingdom. He tempted Christ to choose self-will. Jesus shows that establishing His Kingdom requires **trust, obedience, truth** and **suffering** rather than self-will and independence. As the promised seed of the woman (Gen. 3:15), Christ would have His victory, but only in God's way.

Jesus' entire life and ministry must be understood in light of the conflict between Satan's kingdom and God's kingdom. It is quite significant that many of Christ's miracles were performed in the lives of people possessed by demons, proving His authority over Satan. It was necessary for Christ to demonstrate that His power and authority as King exceeded that of Satan's whose rule over earth was a **rebellion** that began at the Fall (Mk. 3:23-29).

Throughout Christ's life, Satan repeatedly attempted to harm Him, beginning at His birth (Matt. 2:3-8, 13-23). Very frequently, following visible proof of Jesus' authority, an attempt was made on His life (John 5:18; 7:1, 25; 8:37; 11:47-51). Satan carried on his relentless warfare in an attempt to prevent Christ from taking His appointed throne in the kingdom.

Thus, the gospels begin with the King. He entered human life miraculously, fulfilling several Old Testament prophecies. At the same time, those involved with his arrival proclaimed by inspiration of the Spirit that He would fulfill the unconditional covenants God had promised to Israel. At the start of His ministry, Christ dedicated Himself to the Father's will and work of vindicating God's glory and restoring His rule on earth. The Son then engaged Satan in their first of many conflicts. This sets the scene for the ministry of Jesus, the Son of David, Son of Man, and Son of God. He is the long-promised Redeemer-Ruler.

3A. THE GOSPELS AND THE PROGRAM OF THE KING

1B. The Offer of the King and His Kingdom

During his ministry, Jesus offered the Kingdom to both individuals and the nation of Israel. He explained the true nature of the Kingdom and of entrance into it. Proper interpretation demands that you understand that entering the Kingdom differs from inheriting the Kingdom. To **enter the kingdom** is to become a citizen of the Kingdom and comes by **Faith in Christ** as Forgiver (John 3:1-8). To **inherit** the Kingdom is to **share His future rule** and is **a reward** for faithful service (Mk. 10:17; Lk. 18:18).

In John 3, Jesus offered the kingdom to an **individual** named Nicodemus. It is necessary for a person to be born again to see or enter Christ's kingdom and to receive eternal life. Both are obtained by faith. The benefits of Christ's work are received by believing or trusting in Him: "For God so loved the world that he gave his only begotten Son, that whoever *believes in him* should not perish, but have everlasting life" (John 3:16).

In Matthew 5-7, He said the same thing to the **nation of Israel** in the Sermon on the Mount. There, Jesus gave His standard of righteousness for the kingdom: "Unless your righteousness surpasses that of the Pharisees and the teachers of the law, you will certainly not enter the kingdom of heaven" (Matt. 5:20). The Pharisees and Israel's teachers thought that God accepted them because of their circumcision, knowledge of the law and their many traditions. But Jesus said, in effect, "This is not enough. You must be born again. You must have the inner righteousness that I alone can give." In Matthew 5, Jesus taught that outward conformity to moral traditions is not enough. God requires an inward conformity to the law as required in the Land Covenant. In Matthew 6:1 – 7:23, He said that religious activities are insufficient, for the proper attitude makes the proper act right. He concludes by summoning the listeners to embrace his message. This teaching brought Him into sharp conflict with the scribes and Pharisees.

2B. The Validation of the King and His Kingdom: **Miracles** (John 10)

How could individuals or the nation verify that Jesus' message was correct? What proof did He offer for His claims to be the long-awaited Messiah? In Israel's past God used miracles to validate his messengers and message. **Moses** was authenticated by miracles (Exod. 3:20; 4:19,30; 7:10-13). Later, **Joshua** was validated by miracles (Josh. 3:7 – 4:13). Centuries afterward, God confirmed both **Elijah and Elisha** by miracles (1 Kgs. 17:17-24; 2 Kgs. 2:14-15). Jesus' ministry also was validated by signmiracles. They were done to **validate or prove He was the Messiah**, to **demonstrate His authority** as King over all realms, and to **preview kingdom conditions** (Matt. 11:1-6 – verse 5 quotes Isa. 35:5; Heb. 2:1-5, John 5:30-47 – see especially verse 36; 10:33-39; 14:10).

Pentecost writes, "In stilling storms He showed His authority over the earth. In healing the sick He showed His ability to remove the results of the curse. In raising the dead, He

showed He was the Author and Giver of life. In forgiving sin, He demonstrated that he could deal with that which separated men from God."[6]

Christ gave Israel both His words (cf., John 8:28 and 14:10) and His works to validate His offer of the Kingdom. The message and its proof went out throughout the land for almost two years (Mk 1:14-15; Matt. 9:35 – 11:1; Lk. 10:9).

Matthew 9:35 states, "Jesus was going through all the cities and villages, teaching in their synagogues and proclaiming the gospel of the kingdom, and healing every kind of disease and every kind of sickness."

3B. The Rejection of the King and His Kingdom (Matthew 12)

Rather than repenting, Israel rejected Jesus. Rejection began with the **leaders** (Matt. 12:14-37) and eventually ended with nearly the entire **nation** (Matt. 27:19-26). In Matthew 12:25-29 Jesus healed a demon-possessed, blind, and dumb man. The scribes and Pharisees could not deny that the man was healed, but they did not want to attribute this power to Jesus as God or even as a servant of God. Instead, they said that He cast out demons by the power of Beelzebub, the prince of demons (Matt. 12:22-29).

This was a major ***turning point*** in Christ's ministry. Representing the nation, the religious leaders rejected Him as the promised Son of David. This took place about two years before the crucifixion. For almost two years, Jesus

---

6. Pentecost, 207

and His disciples had preached that the kingdom of heaven was at hand. Because the religious rulers attributed His miracles to evil powers and rejected Him as the Messiah, the character of His ministry changed. From now on, Jesus only offered life to **individuals** (Matt. 12:46-50). He also revealed new facts about the kingdom in a series of parables. The kingdom was no longer "**at hand**." The offer of the kingdom was withdrawn and the coming of the kingdom delayed.

4B. The Instruction of the King to His Disciples about His Kingdom

Jesus taught the disciples extensively to prepare them to continue His work after He returned to heaven. We will summarize three key teaching elements.

1C. The <u>Delay</u> of the Kingdom: <u>Mysteries</u> of the Kingdom (Matthew 13)

Because the leaders rejected Him, Jesus began to teach through parables. When he taught the "mysteries of the kingdom of heaven," He taught things previously unrevealed in the Old Testament about the Kingdom. The Kingdom had been clearly revealed in the Old Testament. What was new about the mysteries of Matthew 13 was His postponement and the new truths revealed regarding what would happen between its postponement and realization. These are the parables

of Matthew 13, the "mysteries" or "secrets" of the Kingdom.

The primary point is that the inauguration of the earthly Kingdom will be delayed. There will be an interim period between Israel's **offer** of the Kingdom and her **reception** of it. This interim age began at Christ's rejection and will continue until His return to earth. The rest of Jesus' earthly life, the church age and the Tribulation all belong in the period described as the "mysteries of the kingdom of heaven." Below are summaries of the parables in Matthew 13.

	THE PARABLES OF THE MYSTERIES OF THE KINGDOM	
1	There are varied individual responses to the message of the Kingdom during the interim	13:1-23
2	Satanic counterfeits will live among Kingdom sons and daughters until the end of the age	13:24-30,36-43
3	The interim kingdom will start small but grow globally	13:31-42
4	The interim kingdom will grow by inner dynamic rather than external power	13:33
5	The kingdom is of such value, it should be our overwhelming motivation	13:44-46
6	The interim age ends with a separation of the righteous from the wicked who will be judged	13:47-50
7	Some features of this era are new while others are identical to OT revelation	13:51-52

2C. The Olivet Discourse: The <u>Future</u> of Israel

(Matthew 24-25)

Christ cursed Israel three times because they rejected Him as Redeemer-Ruler (Matt. 11:20-24; Lk. 21:22-24; Matt. 23:37-38; 24:2). These curses pronounced further Gentile domination and the second destruction of Jerusalem and the Temple. The disciples must have wondered if the future held anything good for Israel. Jesus spoke to this in Matthew 24-25 in what is often referred to as the Olivet Discourse. This teaching is about **Israel's future, and not the church**. It is strictly a Jewish message and does not refer to the Rapture or the church in any way. The table below summarizes it.

THE OLIVET DISCOURSE	

The Tribulation Period (24:4-26)
    The first half (24:4-8)
    The second half (24:9-14
    The Antichrist (24:15-26)
	The Second Coming (24:27-30)
	    Regathering Israel to the land (24:31-51)
	    Judgment of Surviving Israelites (25:1-30)
	    Judgment of Surviving Gentiles (25:31-46)

3C. The Upper Room Discourse: The ministry of the <u>Church</u> (John 14-17)

After Israel's rejection, Jesus predicted that He would (in the future) build His church (Matt. 16:13-20) after which would come His Kingdom (Matt. 16:24-17:13). On the night He was betrayed, after He dismissed Judas and initiated the Last Supper, the Lord taught the disciples many things about their ministries in the church after His departure.

The concepts He taught in the upper room are developed throughout the epistles. It is like a garden from which the doctrinal and practical truths of the letters grow. It can be simply summarized as:

THE UPPER ROOM DISCOURSE John 13 - 17	
Relate to One Another with forgiveness, **service** and love	13:1-30
Anticipate Jesus' **return**	13:31-14:4
Believe Jesus' Word	14:5-15
Relate properly to the Holy Spirit	14:16-31
Depend on Jesus for Fruitfulness	15:1-17
Witness to the **World**	15:18-16:11
Understand the **Word** by the Holy Spirit	16:12-33
Jesus Sovereign Care for All Believers	17:1-26

His teaching ministry largely over, Jesus then ratified the New Covenant through His death and resurrection.

4A. THE GOSPELS AND THE PASSION OF THE KING

In theology, the word "passion" means "suffering". The term is often used to refer to the last week, or at least the last several days, of Jesus' earthly ministry leading up to His crucifixion.

1B. The King's Trials

Pilate tried Christ as a **king** (Matt. 27:11; Mk. 15:2; Lk. 23:3; John 18:33) while the Jewish people followed the lead of their leaders as they **rejected** Him as king John 19:14-15 states:

Now it was the day of preparation for the Passover; it was about the sixth hour. And he said to the Jews, "Behold, your King!" So, they cried out, "Away with *Him*, away with *Him*, crucify Him!" Pilate said to them, "Shall I crucify your King?" The chief priests answered, "We have no king but Caesar."

2B. The King's Crucifixion

Although declared innocent six times by both Pilate and Herod, Jesus was delivered over to death. According to Roman custom, the charge for which a criminal was being executed would be prominently displayed. Pilate therefore had the charge written in Aramaic, Latin and Greek: "Jesus of Nazareth, the King of the Jews" (John 19:19-20). The Lord's death accomplished many things, chief among them are:

- Israel was delivered over to **judgment** (Lk. 23:26-32). The kingdom is postponed until that day when a redeemed Jewish remnant cries: "Blessed is He who comes in the name of the Lord" (Matt. 23:39).

- Jesus' death **fulfilled** the promise of Genesis 3:15 (John 12:30-33; Heb. 3:14; 1 John 3:8).

- He paid the sin debt of all men and provided righteousness for all who **trust** Him (Rom. 3:21-26).

- Christ's death **concluded** the rule of Law as indicated by the tearing of the Temple veil. Now, all believers have access to God and worship with acceptance before Him through the New Covenant (Matt. 27:50-51; Rom. 5:2).

- Finally, Jesus death was the first step in the resurrection of all men (Matt. 27:51-53; 1 Cor. 15:20-22).

3B. The King's Resurrection

With Jesus' death, it **appeared** that Satan and his false kingdom had triumphed over the true King. Christ's resurrection, however, proclaims His victory over Satan and the spiritually dark kingdom. It guarantees the eventual establishment of Jesus' kingdom here on the earth – that realm over which the prince of darkness now rules (Matt. 4:8-9; Lk. 22:53; 1 John 5:19). God views the resurrection as His installation of Jesus as His King (Ps. 2:4-9; Acts 13:33; Rom. 1:2-4).

To better prepare for what is coming next, read chapter ten (10) in this resource as well as Ephesians 3 and 2 Thessalonians 2.

CHAPTER 9 REVIEW/SUMMARY

1. John the Baptist prepared Israel for the coming of her long-awaited Messiah/Christ. John's message was "repent" and "behold the Lamb of God".

2. Jesus' baptism by John was for reasons far different than others baptized by John and far different than believer's baptism.

3. Jesus' victory over temptation further validated His claims as Israel's Messiah.

4. Jesus' miracles were done not only to aid people but also to validate His claims to be Messiah, to demonstrate His authority over all realms, and preview kingdom conditions.

5. Jesus was rejected as king by Israel's leaders and later the populace. Afterwards, He began to teach primarily using parables, to reveal new truths to those who did believe.

6. The Olivet Discourse (Matthew 24 & 25) reveals Israel's future in greater detail, while the Upper Room Discourse (John 13-17) reveals the future ministry of the church.

Chapter 10: ACTS AND THE EPISTLES
30 – 100 A.D.

1A. PROGRESSIVE REVELATION IN ACTS

1B. Acts is a book of Transitions

Geographical transitions abound. It begins in Jerusalem and ends in Rome. The gospel went from Judea to the capital of the world in three decades. The church began in Jewish Jerusalem and gradually the primarily Gentile fellowships in Antioch and Ephesus take on more importance.

Acts also records **theological** transitions. There is a dispensational change in Acts from Law to Grace. The long rule of Law ended with the death of Christ. The new age, characterized by grace and the Holy Spirit, began on the Day of Pentecost when the Holy Spirit came to permanently indwell all believers. As part of the promise of the New Covenant, the exalted Jesus now unites all believers with Himself and one another through Spirit baptism (1 Cor. 12:13).
Compare the two ages below.

The Mosaic Covenant focused God's kingdom purpose in a single nation, Israel. It is critical to realize that you were never under Law and that its regulatory aspects never specifically apply to you.

THE DISPENSATION OF LAW	
Israel's Responsibility	**Israel's Failure**
1. To meditate God's rule to the whole earth via Israel (Exod. 19:1-5). 2. To be an earthly kingdom of priests (Exod.19:6). 3. To trust God's promises to Abraham (Gal. 3:15-18)	1. She failed to meditate God's rule globally. 2. She never became a kingdom of priests. 3. She trusted works of the Law rather than God's grace through faith.
God's Judgment on Israel	
He scattered her among the nations. See Deut. 26:16-30:10 and Lev. 26	

The dispensation of Grace, sometimes called the dispensation of the Church, is based on the New Covenant. It delegates God's authority to Christ who is the Head of a universal body, the Church (Eph. 1:21-23).

THE DISPENSATION OF GRACE	
Church's Responsibility	**Church's Failure**
1. To disciple all nations (Matt. 28:19-20, etc.) 2. To reveal Christ through unity (John 17; Eph. 3) 3. To train believers to reign with Christ (Col. 1:12; 3:24).	1. The church fails to disciple all nations. 2. The church is divided. 3. The church is ignorant of Christ's Kingdom program.
God's Judgment on the Church	
The Rapture of the church, leading to the judgment seat, where Christ will evaluate all church saints and determine their fitness for sharing His Kingdom rule (1 Thess. 4:13-18; 2 Cor. 5:9-11). This judgment is not one of wrath or anger. It is rather a just and gracious response to our faithfulness to Him and His purposes.	

In the early stages of Acts, God reveals a second program, the church, operating concurrently with the **re-offer** of the kingdom to Israel. The offer of the kingdom began with John the Baptist's ministry (Lk. 16:16), but Israel rejected it. The King Himself offered it but was spurned and crucified (Matt. 12:22-37; 27:20-26, 37). Throughout Acts, literally from the first paragraph

to the last, God's kingdom and King is the subject. Observe the following verses: Acts 1:3,6; 28:23,31.

To these He also presented Himself alive after His suffering, by many convincing proofs, appearing to them over a period of forty days and <u>speaking of the things concerning the kingdom of God</u>. *So when they had come together, they were asking Him, saying, "Lord, is it at this time You are* <u>restoring the kingdom</u> *to Israel?" Acts 1:3, 6*

When they had set a day for Paul, they came to him at his lodging in large numbers; and he was explaining to them by solemnly testifying about the kingdom of God and trying to persuade them concerning Jesus, from both the Law of Moses and from the Prophets, from morning until evening.
…<u>preaching the kingdom of God</u> *and teaching concerning the Lord Jesus Christ with all openness, unhindered. Acts 28:23, 31*

Christ is the resurrected Son of David who will reign in the future. He is Savior who forgives and gives the Holy Spirit through simple faith. He is the One who will restore all things and fulfill Israel's promises and He is the light to the Gentiles. After Pentecost, Peter made the first re-offer of the King and His kingdom. The Kingdom, the King and repentance go together; Israel cannot receive the Kingdom without it (Acts 2:14-41, Deut. 30:1-10). The re-offer continues throughout the early chapters of the book of Acts.

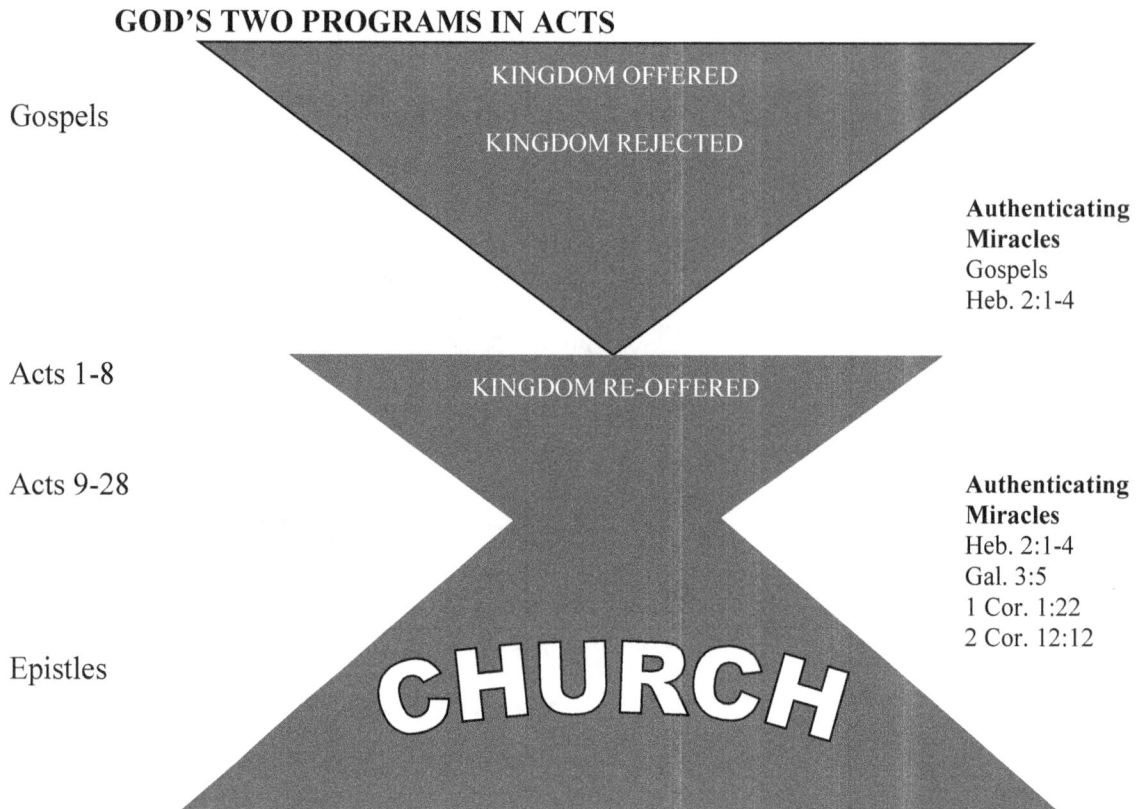

2B. Miracles in Acts

Jesus performed many **sign-miracles** as He offered the Kingdom to Israel, as part of His credentials (Matt 11:1-6). In Acts, the apostles performed the same type of sign-miracles as they re-offered the Kingdom to Israel. Their miracles were signs of their God given **authority** and message (2 Cor. 12:12; Heb. 2:3-4). Chronologically, the miracles of Acts 28:8-9 are the last on record (remember we are referring to sign-miracles, and not all miracles), and the later epistles are totally silent concerning them. With the rejection of the kingdom by the nation in Israel and the Jews of the dispersion, the sign-miracles ceased.

The writer of Hebrews also confirms the fact that Christ's pronouncement that He was the King, and the Kingdom was at hand, was confirmed by miracles (Heb. 2:3,4). It is important to see that there is a relationship between the sign-miracles and the **Kingdom** rather than associating them with God's second program, the **Church**. Of course, this does not mean that God cannot perform miracles in any age. We do not question God's ability to perform miracles in any age in response to faith or prayer or because of His own desires.

3B. The Changing Message in Acts

It is significant that during the forty-day period between His resurrection and ascension that Christ taught the disciples about the Kingdom (Acts 1:1-5). Later in Acts, the church is more in view. The messages recorded in Acts display this transition from a primarily Kingdom message to a primarily salvation one (see chart on next page). Note the early emphasis on the re-offer of the Kingdom to Israel while the message gradually turns to one of **individual salvation** by grace through faith in Christ. After Acts 5:32, the Kingdom promise to Israel is mentioned, but the emphasis falls on individual salvation rather than national deliverance. As the Jews repeatedly rejected the King and His kingdom, the character of the church is more clearly revealed and understood. The Kingdom offer is gradually replaced with the gospel of grace to the Gentiles, including the promise of the coming Kingdom and the opportunity to share Christ's reign. God's program for the Church in this age will continue until "the full number of the Gentiles has come in" (Rom. 11:25). When we preach the gospel today, we need to set it in the context of God's plan for history and focus on preparing people for the Kingdom by faith in Christ rather than just going to heaven.

The following chart synthesizes the speeches and sermons in Acts. Note the gradual change away from the King to the resurrected savior.

APOSTOLIC SERMONS & SPEECHES IN ACTS					
TEXT	SPEAKER	AUDIENCE	PLACE	DATE	SUBJECT(S)
1:3	Jesus	Disciples	Jerusalem	May, 33	Kingdom
1:6	Disciples	Jesus	Jerusalem	May, 33	Kingdom & Israel
1:16-22	Peter	Disciples	Jerusalem	May, 33	Selecting Judas' Successor
2:14-41	Peter	God fearing Jews (2:5)	Jerusalem	May, 33	Re-offer the Kingdom (2:30, 2436; Deut. 30) Salvation from national judgment (2:40) Gift of the Spirit (2:38-39)
3:17-26	Peter	Jews in the Temple	Jerusalem	33	The King and Kingdom (Deut. 30, Acts 3:19-21)
4:8-12	Peter	Sanhedrin	Jerusalem	33	Christ is the King/Capstone
4:23-31	Believers	God in prayer	Jerusalem	33	Boldness as proof of Christ's Kingship
5:29-32	Peter/Apostles	Sanhedrin	Jerusalem	34	National repentance by faith in the King (5:31, Deut. 30)
7:51-8:1	Stephen	Sanhedrin	Jerusalem	34	Jesus is the King (7:52, 56)
8:12	Philip	Samaritans	Samaria	35	Gods Kingdom and King
10:34-43	Peter	Cornelius' house	Caesarea	40-41	Resurrected Jesus forgives sins
11:4-17	Peter	Jerusalem believers	Jerusalem	40-41	God graced the Gentiles to believe
13:16-41	Paul	Jews & God fearers	Antioch	48	Jesus is the resurrected King of Israel
14:15-17	Barnabas & Paul	Gentiles	Iconium	49	God lives
14:22	Paul & Barnabas	Young disciples	Iconium	49	We struggle before entering the Kingdom
15:6-18	Peter	Church council	Jerusalem	49	Salvation is by grace through faith for all
15:13-21	James	Church council	Jerusalem	49	The Kingdom comes after the Gentile work
17:22-31	Paul	Athenian philosophers	Athens	51	Repent, God lives and will judge thru Jesus
19:8	Paul	Synagogue attendees	Ephesus	53	About the Kingdom
20:18-35	Paul	Ephesian elders	Miletus	57	I taught you the Kingdom; inherit it!
22:1-21	Paul	Murderous mob	Jerusalem	57	Paul's testimony and call to the Gentiles
23:1-6	Paul	Sanhedrin	Jerusalem	57	Paul's defense of his ministry
24:10-21	Paul	Felix	Caesarea	57	Paul hopes in the resurrection
25:8-11	Paul	Festus	Caesarea	59	Appeal to Caesar

26:1-23	Paul	King Agrippa	Caesarea	59	Hope in the King, Kingdom & resurrection
27:21-26	Paul	Shipmates	Mediterranean	59-60	God will save us all
28:17-28	Paul	Jewish leaders	Rome	60	The King & the Kingdom, Israel's hope
28:30-31	Paul	All who came	Rome	60-62	The Kingdom and the King

2A. PROGRESSIVE REVELATION IN THE EPISTLES

Both the Church and the Kingdom are addressed in the epistles, but the church receives primary focus. The Church is the vehicle through which Christ now exercises His rule. However, it is closely related to the Kingdom. There are many references to the kingdom in the epistles, and we find the term "kingdom" used in three different ways. **First**, it refers to the **millennial** Kingdom to be established at the Second Coming (2 Tim. 4:1; 1 Cor. 15:23-24). **Next**, it describes the **New / Eternal** Kingdom (2 Tim. 4:18; 2 Pet. 3:18). **Finally**, it often refers to the present **spiritual** form of the Kingdom (Col. 1:13-14). **Context** will always clarify the meaning.

1B. Progressive Revelation about the Kingdom in the Epistles

It is significant that during the forty-day period between His resurrection and ascension that Christ taught the disciples about the Kingdom of God. Some of what He taught them is recorded in the epistles, revealing new truths about the Kingdom not found in the Old Testament. Some of this **supplemental revelation** clarified what the Old Testament revealed. The following are some of the major new truths revealed in the epistles about the Kingdom and the Church's relationship to it.

1C. The **mystery of iniquity** and the Role of Antichrist (1 Thess. 5:1-11 and 2 Thess. 2:1-12)

What Daniel revealed about the 70th week is **supplemented** here. The Antichrist will be a military, political and spiritual leader who will proclaim his own deity in God's Temple. He is now restrained by the presence of the church on earth, who is indwelt by the Spirit. Lawlessness will continue to grow and will reach a peak when the man of lawlessness is revealed.

2C. The Two-Stage Return of Christ (1Thess. 4:13-5:11; 2 Thess. 2:1-12)

Christ will return to our atmosphere (in the clouds) for the church at the Rapture (1 Thess. 4:13-18). At the rapture, He will not come all the way to the earth. At the second coming, accompanied by the Church, He will return completely to earth (1 Thess. 5:1-11; 2 Thess. 2:1-12; Rev 19).

3C. The Rapture and resurrection body (1 Cor. 15:52-58; 1Thess. 4:13-18)

People need new bodies to live everlastingly. The members of the Church will receive theirs at the rapture, a removal of the Church from the earth to meet Christ in the air. Dead believers will receive resurrected bodies while living members will be given new glorified bodies. The Rapture will occur prior to the Tribulation because the Tribulation is primarily a Jewish period (cf. Daniel 9:24-27 and Matt. 24 & 25).

4C. The order of the resurrections (1 Cor. 15:20-28)

Paul outlined a resurrection program that began with the resurrection of Christ and will continue with the resurrection of those who are Christ's at His Second Coming. The completion of the resurrection program does not come until after the reign of Christ here on earth following His Second Coming. At the conclusion of that resurrection program, Christ will have delivered up the Kingdom of God (v. 24).

THE RESURRECTIONS AND THE MILLENNIUM

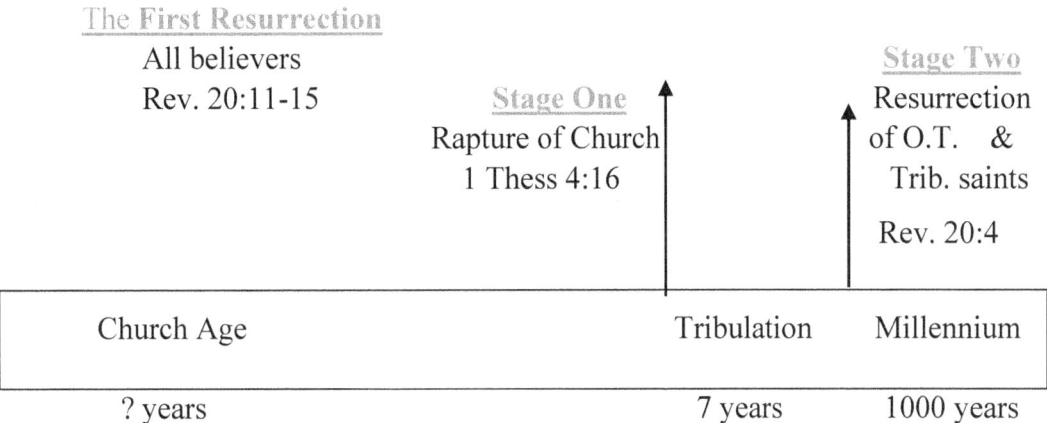

5C. The Church's role in the **millennial Kingdom** (Lk. 19:11-18; Gal. 5:19-26; Eph. 5:3-7).

God intends the Church to reign with Christ in the Millennium (1 Cor. 6:2-3; Rom. 8:17). We are **qualified** to enter the Kingdom and reign by new birth (Rom. 8:17a; Gal. 3:26-29; Col. 1:12-13). However, we must value our birthright to actually share His reign. To share His reign is to **inherit** the Kingdom, which is a reward for faithful, righteous, living in this life (Col. 3:24).

2B. The role of the church prior to the Kingdom

God's present plan includes three basic purposes for the church prior to the coming of the Millennium. The Church is to:

1C. Disciple the Nations (Matt. 28:19-20; Mk. 16:15; Lk. 24:45-49)

Jesus commanded His disciples to take the message of His salvation and His coming rule to all nations. The nucleus of 120 believers formed on the day of Pentecost is the starting point. God's plan is for the Church, through its members, is to preach the gospel in the power of the Holy Spirit and with Spirit-given gifts (Eph. 4:11-16). As people are evangelized and believe the gospel, through the ministry of the Church, they are to be trained so they can enter the same ministries. This builds up the body of Christ both numerically and spiritually.

People are called out from among all nations, with no distinction as to nationality. This is to continue until "the full number of the Gentiles has come in" (Rom. 11:25, Acts 15:13-18). When the body of Christ is complete, Christ will proceed with the Rapture, the next step in His program of undoing the work of the devil (1 John 2:28-3:8).

Before any of the New Testament was written (within 15-70 years of the death of Jesus the entire New Testament was completed), churches were established, and sometimes after only a very short time. Sometimes the church planter (usually Paul in the book of Acts) was only in the place of the church plant for a matter of weeks. Regardless of this perceived obstacle, those churches often flourished and grew without Bibles in their possession or without importing highly trained leaders. A survey of Acts and the epistles reveals five reasons for their success. **First**, Paul and the other evangelists gave the people the key to understanding the Old Testament or its Greek translation – Jesus is *the Christ*. **Second**, their priority was to win the lost and grow the saved. Evangelism, the Great Commission, was a priority, and not a program. It was part of their "DNA" and not an activity. **Third**, they relied upon the gifts and teaching ministry of the Holy Spirit and upon the power of prayer as opposed to their abilities and/or resources. **Fourth**, they emphasized the coming of Christ and His Kingdom. Unfortunately, many churches today rarely, if ever, teach or preach about the rapture and the coming kingdom. **Finally**, they realized the Christian life was a new and different way of life, so they focused on building people rather than buildings (Acts 15:22-36).

2C. Reveal Christ to the World (John 14:9; 17:20-26; Eph. 3:10-11).

Fallen mankind's knowledge of God is perverted (Rom. 1:1823). Jesus came to earth, took on humanity and lived among mankind so that we could learn what God is like. Just before Jesus' death, when Philip wanted Him "to show them the Father," Jesus said, "He that has seen me has seen the Father" (John 14:9). Jesus, by the Holy Spirit, now indwells believers (Col. 1:27; John 14:23) and they are being changed into the image of Christ "from glory to glory, even as by the Spirit of the Lord" (2 Cor. 3:18). Jesus is now revealing Himself to the world through His new body, the Church.

In past ages, God exercised His rule through individuals, Abraham's family and the nation of Israel. Now, the Church is a universal body, comprised of both Jews and Gentiles, united in Christ.

God has done the seemingly impossible, reconciling and uniting the various races in Christ, making the Church the primary display of His wisdom to the various enemy spirits in the heavenly places (Eph. 3:10-11). Christ ascended over these spirits (Eph. 1:20-21), and they now observe His wisdom in the Church. As Christ exercises His headship over the multiethnic Church, He will also exercise headship over all the earth in the future (Eph. 1:10).

3C. <u>Train believers to reign in the kingdom</u> (Col. 1:12-13; 3:24)

We must remember that this age is our **<u>preparatory school</u>** for the age to come (Heb. 12). Our present spiritual training has a direct bearing upon our future service and reward in the Kingdom (1 Tim. 6:11-19; 2 Tim. 2:11-13). In the Garden of Eden, man rebelled against God's order, acting independently of God. Afterwards, all men violated their consciences and rejected God's rule. Israel found that they did not have the ability to keep God's requirements given in the Mosaic covenant. Under the benefits of the new covenant, the Christian has the indwelling Holy Spirit (Titus 3:5-6). We have a new nature through the new birth (2 Pet. 1:3-4). During this Age, we are being trained to walk under the direction of the Holy Spirit (Gal. 5:16) to become like Jesus Christ in character (Rom. 6-8; Gal. 4:19). Only those who are faithful to Christ will reign with Christ (Heb. 2:5-18).

In the parable of the pounds (minas), Jesus said that rewards would be given to servants according to their faithfulness, and that there would be a loss of reward for unfaithfulness (Luke 19:11-28). The rewards mentioned in this parable are responsibilities to rule over cities in the Millennium. There is **NO** indication in Scripture that it will be possible to "play" our way through this life and still expect Jesus' commendation in the future. It is correct to say that spiritual growth is determined by what we do in this life, and this in turn will determine our **position** with Christ in the ages to come. Remember, this refers to positions in the Kingdom and rewards for Christians, but not to salvation. Thus, a key purpose of the Church in this life is to train its members to reign with Christ.

3B. Progressive Revelation about the Christian Life

There are several new teachings revealed about spiritual life that are not in the Old Testament and that apply to only the Church. Among them are the following.

    1C. **Our Position in Christ** (Eph. 1:1)

"Position" is a way to describe what is true of us as God sees it because we are united to Christ. The phrase **"in Christ"** is used seventy-six times from Romans through Jude. It tells us that God, by the Holy Spirit, has joined us to Jesus Christ and applied to us what happened to Him. When He died, we died. When He was buried, so were we. We are raised with Him, seated with Him, and share His authority! (Rom. 6:1-4). Our union with Christ is the basis for our victory over sin. No believers prior to the church age were ever "in Christ." Almost every positional truth has a corresponding practical responsibility. The chart below may help clarify the truth of our position "in Christ."

CONTRAST OF POSITION AND PRACTICE	
POSITION (Justification)	***PRACTICE*** (Sanctification)
Relates to our standing before God	Relates to our walk before men
Is God's instantaneous work	Is the Spirit's progressive work
Is a result of faith in Christ	Is a result of faith and obedience
Is complete, perfect and unchanging	Is incomplete, imperfect and variable
Is the same for every believer	Varies with each believer moment by moment
Makes the believer a saint	Makes the believer saintly
Is the foundation of our growth	Is the progress of our growth

2C. The rule of grace (Rom. 6:14)

The Age of Law ended with the gift of the Holy Spirit at Pentecost (Acts 2:1-36; 11:15-17). At the same time, the Dispensation of Grace began. Because we are in Christ and because He fulfilled the law (Rom. 10:4), we too have positionally fulfilled the law. Therefore, we are not under the supervision of the law. Indeed, we are under the rule of grace, empowered by the graciously given Spirit of God to live in "newness of life" and "reign as kings in life" because of our union with Christ through grace (Rom. 5:17).

3C. **The indwelling Spirit** (1 Cor. 12:13)

The Spirit indwells us because of the New Covenant. The Spirit regenerated believers in other eras/dispensation/ages and He came upon them to temporarily empower them. However, He did not indwell them permanently. This is a special blessing given only to the church. This is true of all believers in this dispensation (Romans 8:9), regardless of how holy or unholy they live, as evidenced by the reality of carnal believers (1 Cor. 3:1-5).

4C. <u>**Inheriting the Kingdom**</u> (Col. 1:12-13; 3:24)

> As co-heirs with Christ by our position (Rom. 8:17), Christians have the possibility of reigning with Him (inherit the Kingdom) in the Millennium. As previously mentioned, He will reward us with various responsibilities in the Kingdom based on our **present** faithfulness. These responsibilities might include the judgment of angels and the world (1 Cor. 6:2-3).

Acts and the New Testament epistles contain much new revelation. Though the Church is distinct from Israel, the King and His Kingdom are still the threads that run through the epistles. Christ has been exalted to the right hand of the Father and given all authority in heaven and on earth. That authority is for the benefit of the Church (Eph. 1:21-23). The epistles describe the purpose and directions for the Church, Christ's body. That body will share His future millennial reign when He completely fulfills the Abrahamic, Davidic, Land and New Covenants. His return and final victory remain to be described in Revelation.

To better prepare for the next section, read chapter 11 in this resource along with Revelation chapters 6-22. Additionally, review the chapter 10 review/summary.

CHAPTER 10 REVIEW/SUMMARY

1. Acts contains geographical and theological transitions. Geographically, Acts transitions from Jerusalem to Rome. Theologically, the transition is from the dispensation of Law to the dispensation of Grace/Church.

2. Early in Acts, the kingdom is re-offered to Israel through Peter. Later in Acts the Kingdom is spoken of less and the primary audience is Gentiles.

3. Supplemental progressive revelation in the epistles includes:
- The mystery of iniquity and the role of the antichrist.
- The two stage return of Christ (rapture then second coming).
- The nature of the resurrection body.
- The order of the resurrections.

4. The Church's role, while awaiting the millennial kingdom, is to disciple the nations, reveal Christ to the world, and train believers to reign in the Kingdom.

5. The position of believers as being "in Christ" is prominent and contrasted with the believer's practice. The former is a matter of justification while the latter is a matter of sanctification.

Chapter 11: THE REVELATION

90 AD -?

"Revelation" means "the **unveiling**" or "the **disclosure**." The book of Revelation is God's final word of special, progressive revelation until Christ returns. Therefore, it is named "**the Revelation**" – it is a single, final capstone to what God has already told us.

1A. THE PURPOSE AND STRUCTURE OF REVELATION

Revelation was written to show us what will happen soon and to provide blessing for those who read and respond to it (1:1-3). Revelation 1:19 says, "Therefore, write the things which you have seen, and the things which are, and the things which will take place after these things." This gives a broad outline of the book. What you (John) have seen (past: Chapter 1); What is now (present - in John's day: Chapters 2 – 3); and What will take place later (future – to John's revelation: Chapters 4 – 22).

2A. THE DISPENSATIONAL CHANGE IN REVELATION

Much of Revelation describes the events of the Tribulation, which is also Daniel's last "week of sevens." This final prophetic week leads up to the coming of Christ and the fulfillment of all the unconditional covenants God made with Israel. A verse that summarizes is Revelation is 11:15 which says:

The seventh angel sounded his trumpet, and there were loud voices in heaven, which Said: "The kingdom of the world has become the kingdom of our Lord and of his Christ, and he will reign for ever and ever."

The Revelation includes the church in chapters 1 – 3, but after this, the church appears to be in heaven. The Rapture concludes the dispensation of grace, so evidently, the covenant between Antichrist and Israel (Dan. 9:27) begins the last dispensation, described as the "age to come" in Ephesians 1:21 and the "fullness of times" in Ephesians 1:10. The following charts summarize this dispensation we call the Millennium and compare the four we have studied.

THE DISPENSATIONS COMPARED					
Dispensation	Covenants	Responsibility	Failure	Judgment	God's Grace
Promise	Adamic Noahic	Believe God & Rule Earth	Submit to Satan Human unity	Fall & Flood Scattering	Promised Seed
Law	Mosaic Land Davidic, New	Be God's Nation	Idolatry	Dispersion	Unconditional Covenants
Grace	New	Disciple Nations	Self-serving	Judgment Seat	Share Kingdom
Millennium	All unconditional	Submit to Christ	Rebel against Christ	Great White Throne	New Kingdom

THE DISPENSATION OF THE MILLENNIUM	
Man's Responsibility	Man's Failure
1. To submit to Christ's rule (Ps. 2, Rev. 20:1-6)	1. Multitudes follow Satan in rebellion (Rev. 20:7-10)
God's Judgment	
There are three final judgments. 1. Mankind is tested, and their sin nature is fully exposed. After 1000 years of a nearly perfect environment, health, peace, productivity, and government, Satan is released for a short period (Rev. 20:7). He deceives the unbelievers from the nations and leads them in rebellion against Christ and His own (Rev. 20:8-9). This demonstrates that mankind's problems are inner problems of nature rather than outer struggles with his environment. Mankind is sinful. 2. God destroys the rebels with fire and assigns Satan to the lake of fire (Rev 20:10). 3. Christ then judges all unbelievers of history and destroys death and sin. All things are now new (Rev. 20:11-21:1).	

3A. PROGRESSIVE REVELATION ABOUT THE TRIBULATION (4:1-20:3)

According to Daniel 9:27, a prince to come will break the covenant with Israel and desecrate the Temple in the seventieth week. Chapters 4-19 in Revelation detail some events of that last seven-year period of Israel's history under the Gentiles. God's judgments of this era are given several names throughout the Scripture. Among them are the **Great Tribulation** (Rev. 6:17; 7:14), the **day of the Lord** (2 Thess. 2:2-8), and the **time of Jacob's trouble** (Jer. 30:7).

Revelation chapters 4 – 19 are written somewhat thematically, like much Jewish writing. Therefore, it is difficult to know exactly when the judgments described in Revelation 6-19 occur. We do know there are three series of seven judgments: the **seal** judgments (6:1-8:10), the **trumpet** judgments (8:6-11:15) and the **bowl** judgments (16:1-17:21). Each set of judgments becomes progressively worse. The chart indicates a sound chronology of Revelation but is not to be taken as dogmatic. Use it as a starting point for your own studies. The numbers on the left side of the chart are chapter numbers from the book of Revelation.

MAJOR EVENTS OF REVELATION Chapters 4-19				
	Before the Tribulation	First Half	Mid-Point	Second Half
4	Throne in Heaven			
5	Lamb on Throne			
6		**First 6 Seals**		
7		144,000 sealed		Multitudes in White
8			7th Seal, 4 Trumpets	
9				5th & 6th Trumpets
10				Angel & Little Scroll
11		2 Witnesses Preach	2 Witnesses Slain	7th Trumpet
12	Dragon vs. the Child		Michael vs. Dragon	Dragon vs. Israel
13		Beast from the Sea	Worship the Beast	
14				144,000 & the Lamb, 3 Angels, Son of Man is Ready
15				Worship in heavenly Temple
16				**7 Bowl Judgments**
17		Great Harlot Rides	Great Harlot Dies	
18				Babylon Destroyed
19				Lamb's Marriage Armageddon

4A. PROGRESSIVE REVELATION ABOUT THE MILLENNIUM (Rev. 20:4-6)

God, through John's pen, prophesied about Satan's final attempt to rule earth through a **false trinity** in Revelation 12-19. The members include **Satan** (Rev. 12:9), the **Beast or Antichrist** (Rev. 13:1-10), and the **second beast** or the **false prophet** (Rev. 13:11-17, 16:13). Although Satan tries to usurp God, he is defeated by Christ and God the Father (Rev. 11:15-19). At the end of the Tribulation, the antichrist and the false prophet are thrown alive into the lake of fire (Rev. 19:19-21) while Satan is seized and imprisoned for 1,000 years (Rev. 20:1-3). As Satan and his minions are defeated, God also destroys their earthly headquarters, which is rebuilt Babylon (Rev. 18:1-24; Zech. 5:5-11).

At Christ's Second Coming to earth and soon after His victory at Armageddon, the first resurrection is completed. By this time, all believers of history will be resurrected (Rev. 20:4-6; Dan. 12:13). The church was previously raised at the Rapture (1 Thess. 4:13-18). Believers who survive the Tribulation enter the Kingdom and enjoy Christ's earthly reign for 1,000 years (Matt. 25:31-46). Israel dwells securely in her land while believers from the nations begin to repopulate the earth and pursue their national life.

Finally, Israel will realize all her unconditional covenants! Abraham will receive all the promises made to him (Lk. 1:55, 73; 13:48; Rom. 4:13). His descendants, Israel, will gain the New Covenant blessings, as they will all be converted (Rom. 11:25-27). The Davidic Covenant will be fulfilled as the resurrected David reigns from Jerusalem (Ezek. 34:24; 37:24-25 and 44:3). Israel will finally enjoy all her land fully under the Land Covenant (Gen. 15:19-21; Amos 9:13-15). And finally, the Mosaic Covenant will be realized as the entire nation of Israel, empowered by the New Covenant, serves God as a kingdom of priests (Isa. 61:6). Note the chart that follows.

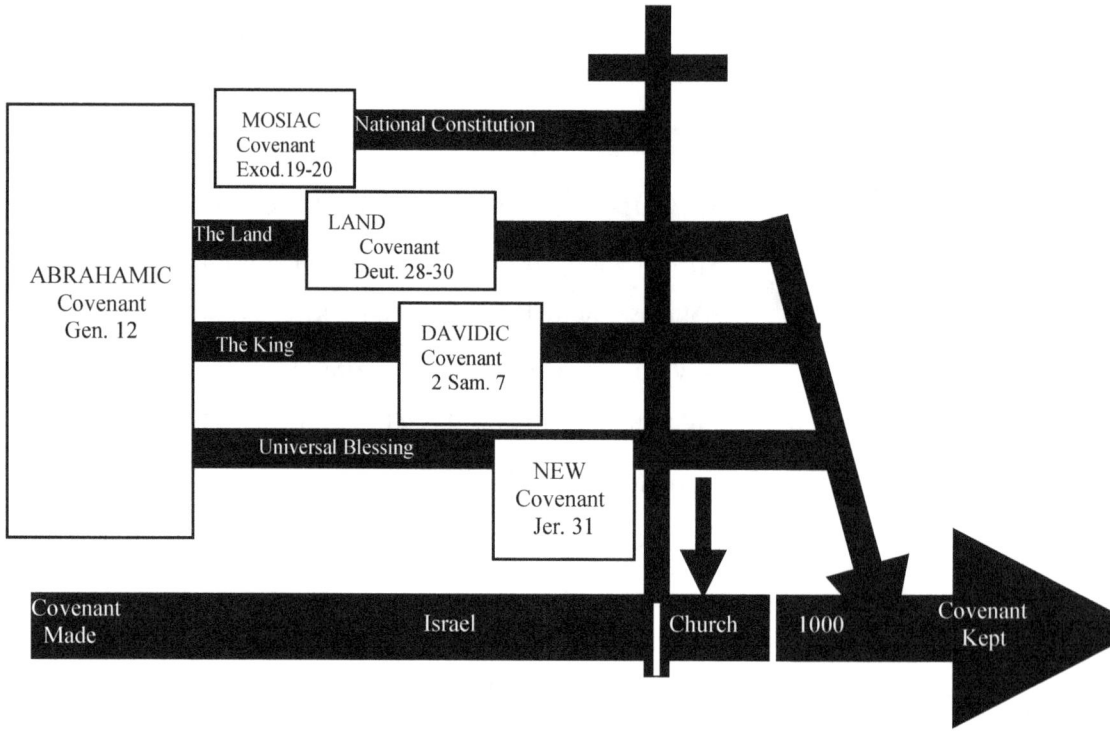

5A. PROGRESSIVE REVELATION ABOUT THE NEW KINGDOM
(Rev. 20:7-22:6)

Throughout the Millennium, God slowly renews the earth and the heavens (Isa. 65:17-20). Mankind lives in a perfect environment under a perfect government. However, all is not well. Sin is not yet done away with.

Tribulation saints who survive will enter the kingdom with physical, nonglorified, bodies. They will parent children, some of whom will not believe the gospel. They will merely conform outwardly to the King's authority. After the Millennium, Satan will be released from his prison. He will deceive these unbelievers into thinking they can rule better than Christ can if they follow him. Satan will lead a final rebellion against God and His people (Rev. 20:10). God will destroy them and cast Satan into the Lake of

Fire. He will resurrect all the unbelievers of history and judge them. They will be condemned at **the Great White Throne** and cast into eternal punishment in the Lake of Fire (20:11-15). Now the final purging of sin is complete. The heavens and the earth are "new."

With sin finally and forever put away, God's righteous rule on earth will be realized, and all the earth filled with His glory. All that He intended in the garden, and more, will be realized. There will be an earthly and a heavenly Jerusalem (Rev. 21). The nations of the earth will walk in submission to the great King (Rev. 21:26). The Tree of Life will keep the unresurrected and unglorified bodies of tribulational and millennial survivors fit for eternity (Rev. 22:1-2). The resurrected ones will share God's eternal rule (Rev. 22:3-5). It will truly and finally be the perfect place and time that man has always looked for and longed for.

6A. THE END IS BETTER THAN THE BEGINNING

When we began our study, we said that to demonstrate His sovereignty, God must defeat Satan, destroy his false kingdom and restore his theocratic rule **where it was usurped**. To restore His rule, God must reverse the six events that man's sin caused, and He must do so **on earth**. Let's see if God does this.

1B. All humans on earth are spiritually **alive** after the Millennium (Rev. 21:4-6; 22:3-6)!

2B. Physical death is abolished after the Millennium (Rev. 21:4)! Imagine, no more death, ever!

3B. Mankind governs earth under God after the Millennium (Rev. 21:6; 22:5)! Remember, God originally created mankind to rule (Genesis 1:26-28). Finally, that purpose will be realized!

4B. God reverses the effects of sin on earth after the Millennium (Rev. 21:4)!

5B. All kingdom subjects are free from Satanic influence and belong to God's kingdom after the Millennium (Rev. 20:10)!

6B. Satan is dethroned, and God's earthly theocracy reestablished forever after the Millennium (Rev. 21:1,2; 22:3)!

Indeed, the Bible is bound together by God's intent to reestablish His earthly rule and express His will on earth in a righteous Kingdom through a righteous King. The chart that follows depicts the overall conflict between God's Kingdom and Satan's counterfeit.

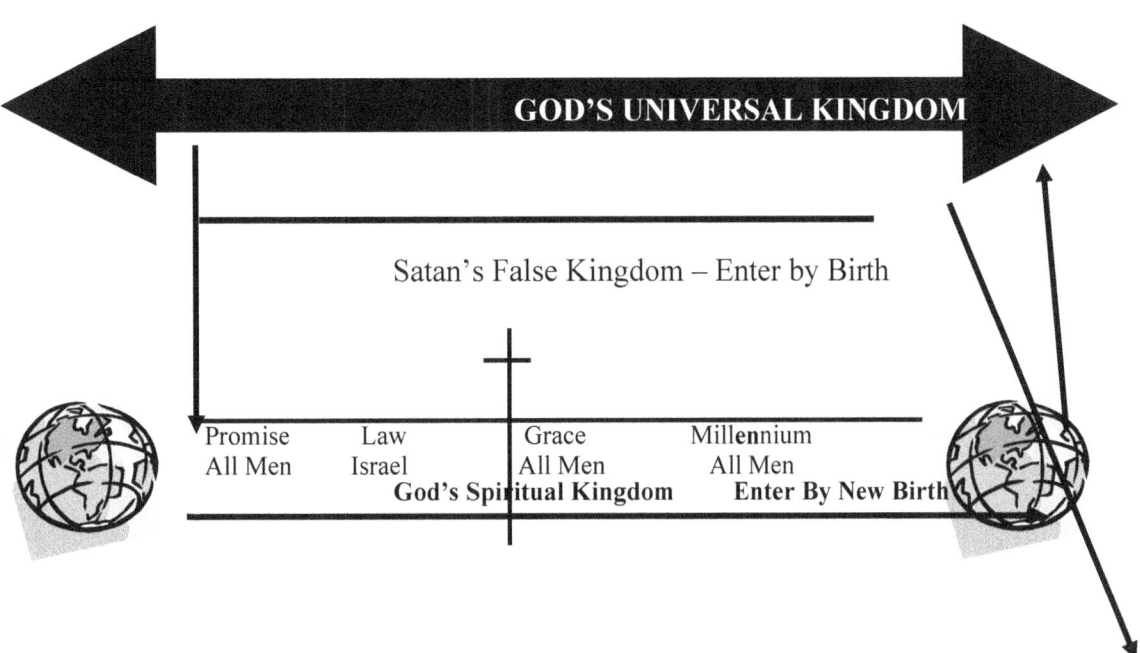

The following chart summarized the progressive revelation about God's plan and purpose to reestablish His righteous earthly rule and vindicate His glory.

PROGRESSIVE REVELATION ABOUT THE KINGDOM		
The Unifying Theme of the Bible		
Ruler	**Realm**	**Responsibility**
Adam	Creation	Man was to obey God and subdue nature.
Noah	Humanity	Administrate justice and guard the sanctity of life through government.
Abraham	His Family	1. To father a nation through who God will one day rule the world. 2. God promised him (a) Land, (b) Posterity, (c) Blessing
Moses and Judges	Israel	1. God was King; Israel the subjects; the Law the constitution 2. Israel was to meditate God's truth to the nations. 3. God appointed judges to rule Israel as needed.
David and Kings	Israel	1. David meditated God's rule to Israel. 2. God promised him (a) dynasty, (b) throne, (c) Kingdom, (d) Everlasting Rule.
Prophets	Israel	1. Called the Kings and people back to the Mosaic Covenant. 2. Announced God's judgment on Israel and Israel's enemies. 3. Prophesied about the final from of the Kingdom.
Gentiles	Israel	After the monarchial kingdom was destroyed, God placed Israel under his discipline via four Gentile empires, the Babylonian, Medo-Persian, Greek and Roman. This is the "times of the Gentiles" and will continue until Christ returns.
Christ	Offered to Israel	Israel was to repent and receive her King. She rejected Him and so has been place aside from blessing for a time.
Christ	Church	The church, ruled by Christ, is to disciple the nations and prepare believers for the Kingdom.
Christ	Millennium	Christ will judge the earth and establish His promised Kingdom in Israel. He will rule earth from Jerusalem.
God the Father	New Kingdom	Christ will turn a new kingdom, that includes a new heaven and earth, over to God the Father.

So that He might localize His rule and to enjoy fellowship with others, God created the universe and populated it with rational beings. Those beings on earth were made in God's image and were designed to rule earth under His oversight. A perfect mini-theocracy existed in Eden under Adam's rule. Lucifer, an angel, rebelled and then enticed Adam to live independently of God. Man chose to rebel, and Satan's false earthly kingdom began.

God forgave Adam's rebellion, but forgiveness only removes guilt, and not the consequences. Therefore, God graciously promised a coming Redeemer /Ruler to fulfill His program, rescue mankind and destroy Satan. God then demonstrated His authority by subjecting all men to the rule of conscience based on God's promise of the Seed to come. Satan helped corrupt mankind's conscience so that man's thoughts were always evil. God then destroyed the human race, except for one family, with a flood.

With that one family, God began a new method of rule, which was a human government. Government was to punish lawlessness and promote righteousness over all the earth. Instead, man again rebelled against God's administration. They built a city that became the earthly center of Satan's rule. In response, God demonstrated His authority by scattering mankind over all the earth.

From these scattered nations, God chose one man and made an unconditional covenant with him. In this covenant, God promised that a great race would come from the man's loins, that he and his descendants would possess a certain land forever and that God would establish His eternal kingdom in that land and from that people. This promise, the Abrahamic Covenant, was confirmed and enlarged through three other covenants, the Land, Davidic, and New Covenants.

God fulfilled His promise as Israel became that chosen nation. God established her as His people on earth and ruled her through His law. Israel forsook God and abandoned His law. In so doing, they brought God's judgment upon themselves. God continues to rule Israel by the Gentile nations under His discipline.

In due time the One whom God promised in the garden was born but Israel rejected Him as their King. So, judgment again came to Israel. Though God reoffered the promised kingdom repeatedly, Israel continued in unbelief and eventually the Gentiles demolished her as a nation in 70 AD.

Because Israel rejected God's offered Kingdom, Jesus created a new group, the Church. The Church is part of the spiritual kingdom and will continue until Christ transfers it into His father's house. At that time, God will resume

His program with Israel. Those seven years of Great Tribulation will be one of severe divine discipline for Israel and judgment for the Gentiles, during which multitudes will trust Christ. That time of divine judgment will end when Christ returns to earth. He will remove all unbelievers from earth and lock Satan away. Christ will rule His kingdom from Jerusalem for 1000 years.

At the conclusion of the Millennium, Satan will be released and lead one final rebellion. God will defeat and then judge the rebels. Sin and rebellion will be forever removed. Jesus Christ will then turn all things back to God who will rule forever. Thus, Satan will forever yield to God's authority. God rule will be reestablished on this earth, and it will be filled with His glory.

Even so, come quickly Lord Jesus!

CHAPTER 11 REVIEW/SUMMARY

1.	The dispensation of the Church ends in Revelation and the Kingdom age is ushered in.

2.	Details of the tribulation. First revealed in Daniel 9:24-27, are supplemented in much greater detail in Revelation, including the seal, bowl, and trumpet judgments.

3.	Revelation supplements much material about the coming millennium, including the roles of the "false trinity".

4.	Revelation contains supplemental revelation about the New/Eternal Kingdom. It will begin soon after the Great White Throne Judgment.

5.	Jesus, the King, will reverse all the effects of the fall/curse before establishing the New/Eternal Kingdom.

BIBLIOGRAPHY

Baughman, Ray E. *The Kingdom of God Visualized;* Chicago, IL Moody Press; 1978

McClain, J. Alva *The Greatness of the Kingdom,* Winona, IN BHM Books; 2001

Pentecost, J. Dwight *Thy Kingdom Come,* Wheaton, IL Victor Books; 1990

Peters, George H. N. *The Theocratic Kingdom,* Grand Rapids, MI Kregel Books; 1972

Ryrie, Charles C. *Dispensationalism Today,* Chicago, IL Moody Press; 1995

Showers, Renald E. *What on Earth is God Doing?* Bellmawr, NJ Friends of Israel Gospel Ministry; 2003

About the author...

Bill Korver served in local church ministry for 22 years, as an assistant pastor and a church planter/senior pastor. He served as an adjunct professor at Carolina College of Biblical Studies (CCBS) from 1990 until 2003. Since 2004 he has served as the president of CCBS. He holds degrees from Southeastern Bible College (B.A. & M.A.), Luther Rice University (M. Div.) and Liberty University (D. Min.). He is married to Marcia and has three grown children and several grandchildren. He enjoys outdoor projects, hunting as well as reading theology, biographies and mysteries.

www.ingramcontent.com/pod-product-compliance
Lightning Source LLC
Chambersburg PA
CBHW081358290426
44110CB00018B/2412